Also by Wess Roberts

Leadership Secrets of Attila the Hun

Straight A's Never Made Anybody Rich

Victory Secrets
of
Attila the Hun

VICTORY SECRETS

of

ATTILA THE HUN

WESS ROBERTS, Ph. D.

DOUBLEDAY

NEW YORK   LONDON   TORONTO   SYDNEY   AUCKLAND

PUBLISHED BY DOUBLEDAY
a division of Bantam Doubleday Dell Publishing Group, Inc.
666 Fifth Avenue, New York, New York 10103

DOUBLEDAY and the portrayal of an anchor with a dolphin
are trademarks of Doubleday, a division of
Bantam Doubleday Dell Publishing Group, Inc.

Designed by Bonni Leon-Berman

Library of Congress Cataloging-in-Publication Data
Roberts, Wess.
    Victory secrets of Attila the Hun / Wess Roberts.
        p.   cm.
    Sequel to: Leadership secrets of Attila the Hun.
    Includes bibliographical references.
    1. Organizational effectiveness. 2. Success in business.
    I. Title.
    HD58.9.R59   1993
    303.3′4—dc20   92-17777
                                                      CIP

ISBN 0-385-42448-5
Printed in the United States of America
January 1993

10 9 8 7 6 5 4 3 2 1

First Edition

This book is for Justin, Jaime, and Jeremy,
with my sincere hope that they will
always be determined to win the
important battles in their lives.

It is also for Cheryl,
who has helped me through
a number of wars in my life.

Contents

Author's Note

Before writing *Victory Secrets of Attila the Hun*, I reviewed hundreds of pages of the notes on leadership and human behavior that I have made over a period of twenty years while working for organizations in both the public and private sectors. These observations are incorporated in the fictional lectures Attila delivers to his chieftains and warriors throughout this book.

In addition, a few people who were particularly helpful and supportive deserve my special thanks.

I am forever indebted to my friend Hugh Doughtery, a retired Bank of America executive, who was kind enough to discuss with me every concept in this book. During the last eighteen months of his life, General Bruce C. Clarke, a bona fide American hero, taught me invaluable lessons on leadership through our weekly correspondence and in a daylong discussion in his apartment shortly before he passed away. Dr. Roger Kaufman, professor at The Florida State University, has been giving me good ideas for many years—to which I finally listened. As a result, many of his insights are included in the chapter on practical dreaming. In fact, with his permission, I even borrowed the chapter title from his work.

One theme woven through this book is that understanding and relating to people are essential to a leader's success. Dr. Hendrie Weisinger, a Los Angeles–based psychologist, has broadened my understanding of interpersonal communication. And Dr. James Bing Kaye Chin, a Santa Rosa, California, dentist, has mastered the art of "people-effectiveness" and has taught me much.

Another theme woven through this book is the importance of courage, will, and commitment. My friend of twenty years, Lee Allen, is an inspiration. As a child, Lee (with his physician mother and his younger brother) became a prisoner of war when the Philippines fell during

World War II. Lee learned that winners who prevail against all odds are men and women of iron will. I am a better person for Lee's teaching me that attitude plays a key role in leading and winning even if we are at a terrible disadvantage.

I am also grateful for my association with Lloyd M. "Pete" Bucher, captain of the USS *Pueblo* when it was commandeered in international waters by the North Koreans. Like many leaders in the business world, Pete found himself in a serious predicament for reasons beyond his immediate control. He showed us that leaders can continue to perform their duties under the worst conditions and can overcome personal hardships as well.

No person was more influential in and important to the writing of this book than was Ellen V. Roddick. Helping me improve my language and ideas, Ellen worked with me throughout the entire writing process. I am fortunate to have a tutor of her caliber.

I am pleased to be represented by Arthur Pine Associates, an outstanding literary agency. As I recall, it was Arthur Pine who suggested that there are many readers interested in a sequel to my earlier work, *Leadership Secrets of Attila the Hun*. Richard Pine worked out the details with the people at Doubleday. Lori Andiman is another key player on the Pine team. And I get to do the most work. Nevertheless, I thank them all for making it worthwhile.

Among the many people at Doubleday who made important contributions along the way, Steve Rubin is owed my many thanks for his confidence and enthusiasm for this project. I am also indebted to David Gernert, who, in addition to his wonderful editing suggestions, was my comrade and counselor in the writing of this book.

I am also obliged to Cheryl, Justin, Jaime, and Jeremy for their encouragement, help, tolerance, and love while I wrote this book. As with my earlier works, they gave me valuable ideas, insights, and suggestions for revisions.

Finally, I am grateful to the leaders I have worked with who taught me to lead and who risked placing me in positions of authority. They also listened to and helped resolve my problems along the way. To them: "Thanks for everything!"

Preface

Rarely in the business world have uncertainty and opportunity been as intense—simultaneously—as they are at the end of the second millennium. Mergers, acquisitions, leveraged buyouts, bankruptcies, and start-ups abound. Established business adversaries form improbable alliances. The savings-and-loan debacle undercuts the availability of capital for businesses and individuals alike.

Companies downsize at an unprecedented rate—even companies that have no tradition of layoffs. As a result, there is no job security today at any level from executive to blue collar. Only CEOs seem impervious to personal economic disaster. More and more workers are dissatisfied with being handed table scraps while irresponsible senior executives raid the payroll pantry with impunity. Yet avaricious leaders escape accountability and deny their followers proportional raises and bonuses. As a result, the gap between accomplishment and reward has broadened for many conscientious and capable workers. Those excluded from career and financial opportunities look outside the work world for other kinds of satisfaction. American business is in trouble.

Major companies abandon the cities because qualified workers there are scarce, housing is expensive, public schools are failing, corporate taxes are high, crime is ubiquitous, commuting is a nightmare, operating costs are high, and an unfriendly business climate prevails.

Complicating the business picture is a dramatic change in demographics. Our population is aging. An influx of new immigrants from the Third World gathers in ethnic ghettos that are not unlike those of early America. Far too many people in our current work force are neither educated nor trained to provide the job skills now demanded. And a shift in the ethnic, racial, and cultural composition of the work force pressures managers to exercise greater interpersonal skills than were needed in the past.

Competition for domestic and foreign market share is fierce. And competition frenzy, which should be guided by moral and ethical rules, instead involves misrepresentation, unfair (protectionist) business policies and practices, crime, blatant disregard for worker safety, cynical indifference to environmental safeguards, and corporate leadership with an "I'll take mine while the taking is good" point of view. In other words, the corruption of American business jeopardizes the nation.

Perhaps not coincidentally, a new lifestyle is emerging among young and middle-aged workers. Fewer of them will sacrifice their health and personal life by giving all their time and energy to the company. More of them turn down promotions that require relocating or giving up valued aspects of their nonwork life. These new attitudes are especially typical of childhood victims of corporate moves who now find themselves without hometown roots. They don't want the transient cycle repeated for their own children; instead, they prefer to remain near their own extended families.

New attitudes about family also affect women who have the potential to become senior executives but who are reluctant to be—or are even opposed to being—deprived of the deep satisfaction of active motherhood. Concurrently, men who missed a strong relationship and shared time with their fathers now focus significant time and attention on their own families.

Uncharted waters lie ahead. The demise of communism brings new hope to millions of oppressed people. It also creates major opportunities for Western business. Technology contributes to the birth, growth, and improvement of many products and services at the same time it threatens our survival as a species. Much is still to be discovered about the responsible application and use of technology.

Unlike military battlefields, where each side seeks its own victory exclusively, the corporate marketplace needs many winners. Every organization must offer job security and career opportunity to workers at every level while providing strong return-on-investment for shareholders. Every country must gain the economic strength to improve its citizens' quality of life. The reduction of abject poverty cannot begin while a few countries dominate the world marketplace. Leaders must learn to share the wealth and prosperity not only with those they lead but with other nations.

This, then, is the business battlefield on which we now fight. The stakes are high. While the rewards of winning often seem elusive, the consequences of losing are dismal. Losing cannot always be avoided, but many of the hazards of business can be reduced. Winning promotes long-term organizational well-being. Winning implies important societal responsibility as well.

I believe the strategies and principles explored in *Victory Secrets of Attila the Hun* not only can increase individual and organizational capacities for winning but also can reduce or eliminate loss on the business battlefields of the nineties and beyond.

Victory Secrets of Attila the Hun is similar in style to my earlier work, *Leadership Secrets of Attila the Hun*. Both are set on the stage of fifth-century Europe, where one man united the Huns and set out to conquer the world. He was Attila, king of Huns.

Politically correct (PC) pundits and historically correct (HC) academicians may wince at my audacity in using Attila —brutal barbarian that he was—as my protagonist. I chose him to guide the reader on an adventure where leaders lead to win and victory is important, because he symbolizes single-minded determination and concern for his followers. Readers will appreciate him if they have the old-fashioned chutzpah to build better products and provide superior service. Readers will see themselves in him if they hire the best people, train them well, develop them into competent workers and managers, provide them with direction, challenge them with responsibilities, reward their individual and group contributions, treat them humanely, and in the process, make a lot of money for themselves, their people, and their investors.

I want to define a few terms used in *Victory Secrets of Attila the Hun* right here at the outset. The first term is *discipline*. Discipline has nothing to do with either corporal punishment or rigidity of mind. Discipline refers either to performing a particular task to specification or else to manifesting a key leadership quality. This kind of discipline evolves as leaders who win improve their organizations. The second term is *loyalty*. Loyalty is not mindless obedience. The best leaders, in fact, suspect anyone who thoughtlessly obeys. Loyalty involves choosing sides and issues you can support. You choose to follow those who lead you because they deserve to be followed. You do the best you can in all aspects of your work. You don't get in your colleagues' way. And when you need help, you ask for it; when you're asked for help, you give it. If you can no longer be loyal in these ways, you need the courage to choose another side. Nothing is worse for a leader than the presence of disloyal followers.

Another point that should be clarified has to do with "perfect" leadership. In this book, perfection is an ideal to work toward but certainly not a goal that can be attained. Leaders have good days and bad days. They have strengths and weaknesses. They get better as they gain experience and maturity. But none become perfect leaders, although some believe they do. Leaders who believe they are above criticism are especially dangerous, for without humility to modulate power, a leader soon loses perspective.

A few additional clarifications need to be made here. First, references to fighting battles and wars are of course to be read as metaphors for competing for markets and market share. Second, fighting is synonymous here with competing honorably through products, service, and price. It does not imply destroying the competition. Third, the battlefield is the metaphorical equivalent of the marketplace. And fourth, victory means successful competition in the marketplace. You should also understand that this book is written from the Huns' vantage point. The Huns are the good guys; the Romans are the bad guys.

At the turn of the third century, the Roman Empire was large and strong. By the beginning of the fifth century, the Roman Empire was like a turtle lying on its back; unless it could right itself, it would perish. The Huns and other barbarian tribes of the late fourth and early fifth centuries were brutal people by today's standards. But the Romans could also be brutal. And today, examples of brutality abound. This book does not rewrite history or justify whatever crimes the Huns or the Romans may have committed against other peoples. But let's remember how difficult it can be to understand the customs and mores of societies different from our own—and how easy it is to feel, unjustifiably, superior to them.

Attila and the Huns versus the Roman Empire—the competition has meaning for us on several levels. For starters, Attila was fun to be around, and the Romans had lost it. Similarly, new business ventures today are high-spirited as they go after markets that old, sluggish corporations believe are securely theirs. Competition seems an affront to the civility of those not accustomed to challenge. In the fifth century as today, the rise of underdeveloped nations challenged the most powerful nations. Then as now, corrupt leaders neglected their people's well-being. Like our times, the fifth century was a very complex period with complexly interrelated events and dramatic turning points. Last but not least, effective leadership qualities are virtually the same today as they were then.

On the one hand, we must remember that the Huns were backward by the standard of their day, yet they united under Attila and to a great extent prevailed over their best competition (the Roman Empire). On the other hand, we must recognize that the hordes who fight to take market share from America's established corporations today are not backward, nor poor in resources, nor uneducated in superior techniques for manufacturing, marketing, and distributing their products. And they are not less determined to win than were the Huns. If a bunch of uneducated savages could hasten the downfall of the mightiest nation in the fifth-century world, imagine how quickly well-financed, well-informed, economically savvy challengers can bring down powerful but inefficient corporations today. None of which means it's time for these corporations to surrender. Quite the contrary. It's time for them to learn from the upstarts. It's time to fight!

Victory Secrets of Attila the Hun is about winning. Winning (making money) is why people go into business. Winning businesses rely on a select number of high-performing individuals who compete at the top of their game. In this book, these people are called warriors. Warriors report to chieftains. The essence of Attila's "victory secrets" is that no tribe or nation can be a continual winner unless it has not only strong and capable leadership (chieftains), but also a sufficient number of competent and competitive warriors— people who make the marginal value-added difference between victory (meeting organizational goals) and becoming a victim. Attila's victory secrets teach that chieftains who bring out the best in their warriors and soldiers lead winning tribes. Winning tribes train promising warriors as potential future chieftains. And chieftains make excellent things happen, set good examples, and disrupt the status quo.

And lest we forget, neither chieftain nor warrior can accomplish much of anything without the help of a few good Huns (soldiers or workers). Altogether too often, "Huns" are treated as if they are nothing more than cannon fodder —insignificant, easily replaced people who can be used and abused with impunity. Such, however, is not the case in *Victory Secrets,* where everyone who serves the Hunnic confederacy is a Hun first and a chieftain, warrior, or soldier second. In fact, as I wrote in *Leadership Secrets of Attila the Hun,* Attila would have said, "There is more nobility in being a

good Hun than in being a poor chieftain." Nevertheless, as
you read, I don't believe you will have any difficulty understanding whether *Hun* is being used in reference to mem-
bership in a group or to identify soldiers who work under
the leadership of warriors.

In *Victory Secrets of Attila the Hun,* Attila is a wise and aged
king who has nothing left to prove to anyone. He reflects on
his triumphs and tragedies without guilt or agony. He
teaches the principles of winning to his chieftains (organizational leaders), warriors (small-unit leaders and senior tech-
nicians), and Huns (nonmanagement workers). The chap-
ters of the book are sequenced so that the historically based
anecdotes that set the scene for each of Attila's last lectures
are in chronological order. These fictional lectures are
counseling sessions in which Attila and his audience gather
around a campfire or in the assembly hall of his wooden
palace in Etzelnburg. They are based on my own experience
and research in leadership. Attila concludes each of his lectures with maxims (Attilaisms) that emphasize key concepts
and summarize the chapter's theme. Attila's lectures focus
on how chieftains develop and lead their tribes to victory.
He includes advice on behavior expected from winning
leaders and on attitudes and behaviors to be avoided.

Although in the stories and in Attila's lectures, leaders
are men, the maxims refer to leaders as being of both gen-
ders. Fifth-century male dominance in fighting wars and in
leading nations and institutions is acknowledged here. So is
the rightful role women fill as warriors today, both in real
wars and in business, government, and society as a whole.
Interestingly, evidence in ancient writings suggests that
women did serve as leaders of Hunnic society. To what extent we do not know. But recorded history was written about
men by men. Histories of Attila were, for the most part,
written by male Roman scribes who would automatically
have excluded mention of women leaders. But readers who
met my "Attila" in *Leadership Secrets of Attila the Hun* will find

that in *Victory Secrets* he is still just a little ahead of his time—
so it is quite natural that he welcomes women as leaders of
Huns and addresses his remarks to them as well as to men.

In the last section of this book, "Chieftainship: 'Leaders'
Diseases and Their Cures,' " Attila speaks to his tribal leaders about infections that threaten them. Some readers may
squirm as they read a diagnosis of their own illness. Others
will find their boss or a difficult subordinate here. The ratio-
nale for this discussion is that leaders need to be warned of
the maladaptive behaviors and rotten attitudes that can seriously impair their ability to fulfill their responsibilities to
their organization.

I hope this book inspires you to contribute with renewed
enthusiasm to the goals and financial strength of your own
organization—and that it stimulates your will to win and
feeds your passion for winning!

PROLOGUE

"Enter the Huns"

The Huns were improbable cast members of the drama played out in Europe in the late fourth to mid-fifth century. The plot included not only their growing power but also widespread corruption, greed, intrigue, civil war, inept leadership, and (perhaps inevitably) the collapse of the once great Roman Empire.

The Hunnic horde comprised Hungarians, Turks, Slavs, Mongols, and Asians who united in the fifth century as a confederacy led by Attila, king of Huns. Attila was probably from an Asiatic tribe that the Chinese called Hiung-nu, which translates as "common slaves." Regardless of how the Chinese saw the Huns, his Huns saw Attila as a member of the royal clan that had provided them with leaders when, as loosely aligned, nomadic tribes, they had roamed the vast Mongolian plain, slowly migrating west.

The Roman Empire included large cities, small villages, and vast estates. Trade was well established. Citizens paid taxes to a central government. In contrast, the Huns lived on their horses, in tents, and in chariots and roamed the plains, surviving off the land. Their trade was limited to horses and slaves taken as prisoners of war. Having no central government, they paid no taxes.

The Huns were as noisy in battle as they were fierce. The pounding hooves of their shaggy plains ponies were accompanied by the roars of the Hunnic cavalry as they charged into battle. Yet the threat the Huns posed to the Roman Empire was negligible for a long time.

The Huns' push westward began in the twilight of the fourth century and went largely unnoticed. Around A.D. 375, the Huns took the Ukraine and forced the Goths to flee to the Pannonian basin. The Eastern Roman (Byzantine) emperor allowed the Goths to settle there under terms of a treaty that required them to provide foederati (mercenaries) to supplement the Empire's ailing imperial army. Later, Huns were to fight side by side with Goths as fellow mercenaries in that army.

The Huns continued their westward migration for the next twenty-five to thirty years, arriving at the eastern edge of the Roman Empire early in the 400s.

The Asiatic Huns looked different from the Caucasian Europeans. They were short, stout, and swarthy, with high cheekbones and dark hair and eyes. Hardened by nomadic life, many Huns wore clothing made largely from animal skins, which enhanced their ferocious appearance. Virtually all Hunnic males were accomplished hunters, horsemen, and archers. No doubt many of the women were as well. The customs and beliefs of the Huns and the Romans bore little similarity.

Neither pagans nor Christians, the Huns revered nature deities and believed in the healing, prophetic, and visionary powers of their shamans. In contrast, a declining number of Romans still worshiped pagan gods, while the majority had converted to Christianity. In the fourth century, Constantine the Great had made Christianity the official religion of the imperial Roman state.

The first Huns to enter the Roman Empire were not bellicose. For nearly half a century, the Huns, like other barbarian tribes, provided mercenaries to supplement the dwindling Roman army. In return, the Huns were allowed to reside on the abandoned fringes of the crumbling Roman frontier.

During this period—shortly after the death of his father,

King Mundzuk—Attila was sent by his uncle, King Rugila, as
a child hostage to the court of Honorius, emperor of the
Western Roman Empire at Ravenna. (The practice of send-
ing child hostages to live among potential enemies was well
established during this period. On the one hand, the children were exchange students. On the other hand, many
hostilities were avoided while these child hostages were in
an enemy's custody.) About the same time, a half-German,
half-Roman boy named Aëtius was sent as a child hostage to
the camp of the Hunnic king, Rugila, in the ancient Roman
province of Pannonia (which became Hunland to the
Huns). Attila's experience at the court of Honorius and Aëtius' experience with the Huns influenced them when as
adults they led their respective nations.

After Attila's departure from Ravenna, he traveled among
the tribes of Huns for twenty years, persuading fiercely independent chieftains to support his plan for a Great Conquest
by a new Hunnic confederacy.

By 434, the Huns had gained enormous power. Attila had
emerged as their co-ruler with his older brother Bleda. Together the brothers negotiated a treaty with Theodosius II
that required the Eastern Roman Empire to pay the Huns a
huge tribute of gold in return for peace. Attila is widely
believed to have murdered Bleda around 445. Another version of Bleda's death attributes it to a hunting accident. In
any event, Attila became the sole king of Huns.

Fighting for the Western Roman Empire, the Huns defeated the Visigoths, the Franks, and the Burgundians.
Meanwhile, Aëtius was caught up in a power struggle with
two other generals that forced him to flee for his life. He
took refuge with the Huns, and King Rugila equipped him
with an army of Hunnic warriors. The imposing threat of
this horde convinced Placidia, who was regent in the West at
the time, to restore Aëtius as *magister militium in praesenti*.
Because of the unusual power afforded the *magister militium
in praesenti* (who was both master of soldiers or supreme
military commander and *patricius* or prime minister in the

West), Aëtius was the real ruler of the Western Roman Empire for much of the period between 433 and his death in September 454. For years, he relied on the Huns to supply him with mercenary soldiers.

Attila's vision for the Huns' future suggested world governance secured by his mighty army, which would be trained according to the Roman model. By the early 440s, the Huns were settling permanent villages and building wooden homes: The king of Huns, known among Germanic tribes as Etzel, established his capital city, Etzelnburg ("the city of Attila"), in Pannonia, probably on the site of the present city of Budapest, Hungary.

During the late 440s, Attila concentrated his attacks on the Eastern Roman Empire. His vast army included not only Huns but also Heruli, Scirians, Rugians, Thuringians, Ostrogoths, Gepids, Burgundians, and Ripuarian Franks. In 451, with Attila in command, this horde crossed the Rhine and swept into Gaul to destroy a number of cities. The Great Conquest had begun.

Attila now refused to provide any more mercenaries to Aëtius. Alarmed—and fully aware of the threat the Huns posed to Italy—Aëtius convinced his former enemies, the Visigoths, to join forces with him and his largely barbarian troops. They succeeded in chasing the Huns out of Orléans. Then the two great barbarian armies—one commanded by Attila for the Huns, the other commanded by Aëtius for the Western Roman Empire—met on the Catalaunian Plains (near present-day Troyes, France). There they clashed in one of the major battles of the Middle Ages, the Battle of Châlons.

The Battle of Châlons was bloody for both sides. Although there is no generally accepted figure for the number of men in either army, it is known that thousands of men and horses were slain. Eventually, Attila retreated, giving Aëtius a de facto victory. The king of Huns then returned to Hunland.

Although the West's victory at the Battle of Châlons was

inconclusive, it convinced Attila that his army needed major reconstruction. With characteristic fervor, he dedicated himself to reorganizing his army. By 452, the Huns that invaded Italy were trained, equipped, motivated, and disciplined as never before in their history.

Aëtius had fallen out of favor with the emperor and the Senate, possibly for allowing Attila to withdraw at the Battle of Châlons. As a result, they no longer sought his advice on dealing with the Huns as was warranted by his office as supreme military commander and prime minister in the West. In addition, a large portion of Aëtius' army that fought the Huns in Gaul had been disbanded. Attila's Italian campaign, therefore, met virtually no opposition from Roman forces, and the Hunnic horde devastated city after city. Their rapid advance was briefly halted at Aquileia, which they razed only after a long siege. Although many Huns were sick and rations were scarce, the horde rode on and destroyed Patavium. The cities of Vicenza, Verona, Brescia, Bergamo, Milan, and Pavia simply opened their gates to the Huns. In return, their citizens suffered fewer atrocities than had those of Aquileia and Patavium, who had stubbornly resisted.

Finally, Aëtius decided he could effectively challenge the Huns when they had been worn down by disease, famine, and the unfamiliar heat of the Italian peninsula. Attila and his horde were resting on the banks of the Po at the same time that Aëtius and his Roman soldiers were camped near Mantua, southeast of Milan. The *patricius* viewed the Huns from a distance and saw many signs that they were weakening at last. Confident that he had little to fear if he opposed the Huns in August, Aëtius rode to tell this good news to the emperor, Valentinian.

Valentinian had fled from Ravenna to Rome to escape Attila's advancing army. There he listened to an altogether different plan to persuade Attila to spare the rest of the Italian peninsula. Several among the emperor's inner circle of advisors believed Attila might respect men of religion, for he had spared Troyes when Bishop Lupus asked him to. The emperor, therefore, asked the pontiff, Pope Leo, to meet with the king of Huns and to appeal to him for peace on behalf of the Empire.

As Aëtius made his way southward to tell the emperor he could soon stop the Huns, he was astonished to see the pope and his retinue pass him. Little did Aëtius know that Leo was on his way to meet Attila near Mantua. Valentinian had not told Aëtius about the papal peace mission to the king of Huns.

The pope and the king met in private on the south bank of the Mincio River. Not long afterward, Attila turned his horde north toward Hunland. Rome was spared.

I

Let a Roman Do It

"Don't Waste Your Energy"

Even before the birth of Attila, the Huns were playing a decisive role in the path of history. By the fifth century, the Roman Empire was little more than a glowing ember of the brightly shining star it had once been. Upon the death of Theodosius the Great (the last emperor to rule a united Roman Empire), the Roman world had been divided, and the two realms had drifted further and further apart.

The Empire had been split into separate dominions before (for efficient territorial jurisdiction), and the senior emperor had been ultimate ruler of the Roman world. But when Theodosius' sons—Honorius in Mediolanum (present-day Milan), and Arcadius in Constantinople (present-day Istanbul)—succeeded him as emperors, their governments went separate ways. As a result, the Roman Empire lost its superior political and military clout.

Political relations between Honorius in the West and Arcadius in the East were often strained. Their leadership was neither brilliant nor inspirational. In fact, both brothers were dullards caught up in court intrigues—of which there was never a shortage. Mere titular emperors whose role was to approve the recommendations of their generals and senior court officials, neither accomplished anything significant during his reign. So much for the worth of "born leaders."

Had the crumbling Empire suffered only from stupid and weak emperors, history might have been different. But in addition to incompetence on the throne, the Empire was undermined by heretical bishops, unscrupulous civil servants, treacherous eunuchs with positions of influence, and rival generals who incited civil wars. Defending the vast frontiers of the Empire and funding insatiably wasteful governments were problems made intractable by the slowdown in the slave trade and the sharp decline in the birthrate. When the rich landowners who needed field workers competed against military leaders who needed soldiers for the available young men of the Empire, the landowners generally won.

To fill the void of native manpower for its armies, the Empire not only recruited barbarians but also forced defeated tribes to supply recruits. The barbarization of the Roman army was not limited to auxiliary units, as in the past. Now many commanders were barbarians. So it came to be that thousands of barbarians, mainly Goths, served as soldiers in the imperial armies. To no one's surprise, among the barbarians who gained prominence fighting for the Empire were the Huns.

In 405, when the Western Empire was trying to recover from the earlier Goth invasions (which it had repelled with difficulty), Radagaisus, a well-known Goth soldier of fortune, decided to wage war on Italy. Leading a horde of over two hundred thousand Germanic warriors, he swept down from the Alps, made his way through northern Italy, and laid siege to Florence. Radagaisus was a nasty and bull-headed leader who boasted that he would slaughter two million Romans—sparing no prisoner. He was impervious to diplomacy and rejected negotiation.

It was a time of great despair for the Romans. They could count neither on the mercy of Radagaisus nor on their own regular barbarian troops—who were too spiritless to turn back this new invasion. With Rome threatened virtually on every side by barbarians, Stilicho (supreme military commander in the West) formed military alliances with Sarus, the Visigoth king, and with Uldin, the Hun king who ruled

Muntenia. The Romans distrusted the Visigoths but valued their military support. Most Romans also distrusted the Huns—small, savage, yellow-faced, and beardless cavalrymen armed with crude, outlandish weapons and speaking an unintelligible tongue. Even as allies, the Huns provoked contempt in Latins. It was a curious attitude for "civilized" and "cultured" people on the verge of being massacred. The bottom line, however, was that the Romans were not too repulsed by the Huns' appearance to refuse their help in an emergency.

Stilicho and his army of about twenty thousand Romans, Visigoths, and Huns engaged the barbarian invaders near Florence and pushed them into the hills of Fiesole. Although Stilicho's regular forces showed but feeble opposition to Radagaisus' cavalry, Uldin led his Huns in a series of dazzling charges. This allowed Stilicho to surround Radagaisus' troops and cut them off from food and water. Physically weakened, more than half of the invaders were slaughtered, and the survivors fled in disorder with the Huns at their heels. The Huns had done for the Romans what the Romans couldn't do for themselves. Radagaisus was captured, taken to Rome, and beheaded.

To show their appreciation, the citizens of Rome honored the patchwork Roman army with a parade. Stilicho, with Uldin at his side, rode at the head of the column. Sarus and his Visigoths brought up the rear. The Roman generals, accustomed to the ingratitude of the people, were astonished when cheering crowds greeted the passing Huns. Silence fell as all others rode by.

This was not the only time the Huns aided the Western Roman Empire. Huns served admirably in a Hunnic garrison at Ravenna. In 425, Aëtius hired the Huns to help his West Roman army when Theodosius II sent his East Roman army to install Valentinian III as emperor in the West. And in 433, an army of sixty thousand Huns accompanied the exiled Aëtius—who was able to convince Placidia to reinstate him as supreme military commander and prime minister in the West. Moreover, Rugila lent Aëtius a Hunnic army to fight with him under Litorius in Gaul.

In return for their mercenary service, the Huns were paid in gold, allowed to keep their prisoners or to sell them as slaves, and occasionally permitted to negotiate territories for themselves that the Romans did not want.

After more than thirty years of fighting for (and in minor skirmishes against) the Romans, the Huns had nothing to show for their efforts. Despite their incredible military strength and fighting spirit, the Huns remained dreadfully poor. Their inefficient method of production trapped them in an exceptionally primitive economy. As mercenaries, they were simply paid to do a job for the Empire and to go home as soon as possible. Outstanding on the battlefield, they were feared by the Romans' enemies but did not alarm the Romans themselves. Because they operated as isolated tribes without political or military integration, the Huns posed no real threat to the Empire. Aëtius was among the very few Romans who felt anything but contempt for the Huns.

As king of Huns, Attila decided nothing was to be gained from their further service as mercenaries to an empire they could surely conquer. After the massacre of Litorius' Huns at Toulouse in 439, Attila put an abrupt end to the supply of Hunnic warriors and armies to the Empire. But his Great Conquest would not begin for more than a decade.

In his later years, Attila spent many hours convincing tribal chieftains and nobles that the Hunnic nation would achieve its greatest potential through unity of purpose. He insisted that Roman military service for the Huns had been a waste of effort and life.

Attila on:
"Don't Waste Your Energy"

My long life's experience has taught me many secrets of winning that I will share with you chieftains this night. When I was young, my father and his brothers ruled our nation and often sold the services of their warriors to the Romans, just as their forefathers had done before them. And at times, they themselves led our Huns on these campaigns. Early in my reign as your king, I, too, honored military commitments our tribal leaders before me had made with the Romans.

However, when so many of our young warriors and soldiers fell at Toulouse, I realized that using our armies to fight for our own causes made more sense than continuing policies of old. Besides, Huns dying in battles for the Romans conflicted with my plan for the Great Conquest.

You have to learn as chieftains that some things are worth a warrior's efforts and some are not. Warriors work in positions of responsibility and visibility that can contribute to the future wealth of our tribes and nation only if they fight for us alone. But our ancestors ignored future goals for present gain and accepted campaign missions from the Romans. So did I, mistakenly believing that a warrior worth his or her weight in booty should fight any battle that paid well. I was wrong!

I have learned that warriors are so important to our tribes and nation that we must not waste their time. Many tasks that must be done for the good of the tribe are too inconsequential to assign to warriors and should be given to Huns. Other tasks, performed within virtually every tribe, aren't worth doing at all. Listen now as I give counsel on the use of a chieftain's, warrior's, and Hun's time.

• Wise chieftains never engage their tribes in marginal battles. It costs too much, and the rewards are usually not worth the tribe's time and energy.

- A warrior's worst fear is that he or she will be assigned a task that the chieftain doesn't want completed successfully.

- Petty events cannot assume importance regardless of how hard a petty chieftain, warrior, or Hun works to magnify them.

- Warriors and Huns are wise to turn down assignments they don't believe they can handle—no matter how great the booty promised by the chieftain.

- Weak chieftains sometimes assign tasks to Huns that are a waste of time. Huns resent being so misused.

- Warriors with high potential turn down assignments that don't offer an opportunity for them to learn and grow.

- Huns should be encouraged to become more effective and efficient, so the experienced chieftain helps Huns identify opportunities to learn.

A chieftain who can't find meaningful work for a warrior or Hun does not find a trivial assignment instead. Rather, the chieftain trades unneeded warriors and Huns to a tribe where they can be productive.

And by way of ending my counsel for you this night:

- When the Romans are eager for Huns to do things Romans should do for themselves, there are two consequences. First, the Empire wins. And second, the Huns lose. I, Attila, king of Huns, have never been keen on losing.

As you depart this gathering, I admonish you to be forever aware that our success as a nation of Huns rests upon what we accomplish in our own interests and not on what we do to benefit the Romans.

II

One Tribe, One Mind

"Tribal Togetherness"

Both their civilized and barbaric contemporaries feared the early Huns. The Hunnic cavalry was amazingly effective with the bow. Attacking in swift circular motions, these fierce horsemen would launch a barrage of arrows that quickly defeated all but the most well-fortified cities. They struck with no objective beyond looting. Intoxicated by adventure and movement, they seemed invincible. Most civilized people considered them reprehensible savages at best, the offspring of wizards and demons at worst. Some clerics even taught that Huns were sent by God to punish the world for its debauchery.

The Huns' reputation was based more in fiction than in fact. As a mysterious horde of unknown origin, the Huns caused panic because they seemed strange, savage, and invulnerable. The Huns who first crossed the Danube into western Europe had vanquished all the nations of eastern Europe—the Alani, the Vandals, the Visigoths. They spoke a language incomprehensible to the Romans and looked more like furry animals than human beings. Earlier, the Germanic tribes that had conquered Rome also seemed to the Romans to be uncouth warriors who loved battle and the rewards of its booty but were ignorant of civilized pleasures. Historically, then, Romans were in the habit of sneering at their enemies, taking the view that to attack the Empire was to attack civilization itself and was, therefore, the most savage of crimes.

The Huns were, to be sure, fierce warriors and primitive nomads. But they were by no means bungling savages when they arrived at the Danube to challenge the crumbling Western Empire. Despite the dark tales the Romans told of Hunnic cruelty and atrocities, the Huns were no more brutal to their enemies than were the Romans themselves. Not yet a nation of Huns, they were more dreaded than they were ferocious. Each tribe was lead by a warrior-chieftain and acted independently. During their wanderings, these vagabonds intermarried and melded into a mixture of Mongol, German, and Scandinavian. One family that remained distinctly Mongol formed the aristocracy of the Huns. Late in the fourth century, its king, Mundzuk, sired a son who would rise to unite a vast and geographically dispersed people into a powerful confederacy that imperiled the Roman Empire. This great leader was, of course, Attila.

Sometime during 407, when Attila was only twelve, King Mundzuk died, and the leadership of his tribe passed to his brother Rugila. Attila criticized his uncle's policies, and King Rugila soon arranged for him to be educated as a child hostage by the Romans. In the palace of Honorius (the ineffectual child emperor of the Western Empire), Attila watched the once powerful Empire grow weak in the fifth century. Treachery, intrigue, greed, and envy corrupted officials, and the glorious nation that had given its citizens and subjects the greatest gift of all—peace—crumbled from within. The Empire's goals were no longer clear and no longer united the nation. Taxes grew increasingly burdensome as government spending soared.

Owners of huge estates lost their fortunes to taxes and war. Inept military policy badly compromised both the army and the navy. Because the birthrate sharply declined at the same time that slaves became less plentiful, the labor force decreased alarmingly. Concurrently, the barbarian birthrate sharply increased, so barbarian tribes began to occupy lands along the Empire's frontier. Not even the highly developed and sophisticated Roman government could rectify all these problems.

By the time Attila completed his term as a hostage and returned to the Huns, he had become a man. He knew the Empire was vulnerable but saw its conquest as anything but certain. His first step must be to unify the Huns, provide them with central leadership, give them national goals of their own, and rid them of Roman military domination. Learning to work and fight together as tribes and as a nation meant that everyone must do his or her part. To achieve unity and teamwork would require all the Huns' best efforts.

Among highly competitive chieftains and warriors, unity of purpose has a fragile existence; it must be constantly fought for, or it will be lost. Attila visited the Hunnic tribes and built support for his long-range plans. In doing so, he forged them into a nation under his own leadership. Even after he became king of all Huns, he never took for granted their loyalty to his central government or their unity of purpose. He chastised rebel chieftains, reminding them that disunity leads to self-defeat for any nation.

In addition to overseeing distant chieftains, Attila had to resolve political difficulties in his own family. Although he had more than sixty sons, he promised kingdoms to only six of them and gave a province to only one of these, Ellak. The five who received promises were jealous of Ellak and wanted to rule over their own kingdoms. Attila did not think they were ready to assume such responsibility, so they became outspoken critics of his policies. His Great Conquest would take time and required the loyalty and teamwork of all his sons as well as of chieftains and other nobles. Only together could the Huns conquer the world. The king of Huns, therefore, met with his six sons and with tribal leaders to instruct them on Hunnic unity.

Attila on:
"Tribal Togetherness"

If we are to break the shackles of poverty and escape our nomadic life, we must unite our tribes in a strong Hunnic confederacy. This will not be easy. All Huns must be convinced that more is to be gained by working together than by fighting one another or by fighting for the Romans.

You chieftains and you, my sons, have pledged your loyalty to the great Hunnic cause. It is now up to you to persuade all warriors and Huns that they will profit by making a similar pledge to our tribes and to our nation.

You chieftains are as vital to our success as are my sons. Organize your tribes to work toward our common goals. Revise your plans and update your organization to ensure your tribe's best performance.

Solicit advice from your warriors and Huns to overcome obstacles and avoid pitfalls. Persuade obstinate warriors and Huns to support the tribal effort—or remove them from the tribe.

I cannot predict all the challenges you will face. But I can offer counsel to aid you in dealing with many of them. And for that purpose, I ask you to heed my thoughts now on achieving tribal togetherness.

- Although warriors prefer independence, chieftains should persuade them to work cooperatively. A unified effort produces superior results.

- A chieftain who consistently inspects the work of the warriors and Huns finds that they consistently produce better results.

- Unless chieftains assign warriors and Huns to jobs that allow them to grow and develop, the talents of both warriors and Huns deteriorate.

- Huns given tasks without deadlines don't get them done.

- One Hun's bad habits can infect other Huns. Likewise, one Hun's good habits can inspire other Huns. Wise chieftains reward the habits they wish the tribe to adopt.

- Many bad habits are formed early in life, so chieftains should pay attention to the activities of young Huns.

- Chieftains who assign two warriors the work of one wastes resources. They also lose the support of warriors who don't appreciate the recognition and rewards that go with doing half a job.

- A bad chieftain usually has inferior ideas and makes poor decisions. The only time good warriors take orders from a bad chieftain is when they don't have the option of teaming up with a good chieftain.

- Lasting bonds between chieftains and their warriors and Huns aren't forged in battlefield triumphs and tragedies. They develop over time as everyday exchanges between chieftains and their warriors and Huns build esteem and tribal well-being.

- Outstanding warriors have a natural arrogance that must be disciplined to benefit the tribe. Achieving cooperation among these stars is a slow, challenging process even for a chieftain of iron will.

- Rebels and grumblers must be chastened or they will undermine tribal unity.

- A warrior never abandons his or her cause. So a wise chieftain makes sure his or her warriors support the tribe's cause.

- If a chieftain ignores top performers, they lose their winning edge. If a chieftain ignores weak performers, they never develop a winning edge.

• A tribe performs at its best when everyone is assigned the tasks he or she does best for the tribe.

• Unless a chieftain takes immediate, decisive action to curtail it, disunity becomes a destructive power that is very difficult to stop.

• Chieftains should never expect to gain more from their warriors and Huns than they give to them in terms of training, mentoring, and appropriate assignments.

• Often when warriors and Huns fail to achieve what is expected of them, their chieftain has failed to convey his or her expectations to them.

• Chieftains who critique past battlefield performances for warriors and Huns increase the odds of winning future battles.

• When all warriors and Huns achieve everything expected of them, their chieftain has set the standards too low. Warriors and Huns come in a full range of talents and ambitions. Chieftains should challenge each warrior and Hun appropriately.

• A chieftain should stop training his or her warriors and Huns only when winning is no longer important. And I, Attila, king of Huns, am at a loss to fathom when winning may become unimportant for any tribe or for the nation.

• Joining tribal efforts in no way diminishes a warrior's or Hun's chance to make a meaningful individual contribution. Rather, joining tribal efforts adds depth and dimension to a meaningful individual contribution.

• Chieftains realize that the success of one warrior or Hun in no way diminishes the achievement of another. Warriors and Huns do well to recognize this fact as well.

Huns who don't know how to fight but have the will and capacity to learn are potentially good Huns.

And now I conclude your counsel with this thought:

• Chieftains create strong morale and discipline in the tribe when they train their warriors and Huns well, tell them what is expected of them, allocate to them the necessary tools and weaponry, and provide them with the leadership required to win.

Go now to your tribes and provide leadership that enables them to fight for victory with a unified spirit, so we can heap on them the spoils of triumph.

III

Managing the Tribe's Cache

"It's Easy to Be Generous with the Huns' Booty"

As a child hostage in Ravenna, Attila developed a keen ability to observe things as they were, not as they appeared to be. In consequence, he gained insights into organizational politics that later served him well as king of Huns.

One of the more deplorable aspects of court life was the greed of the eunuchs and ministers who oversaw tax collection. Attila perceived that only a small percentage of taxes ever reached the imperial treasury. Corrupt officials used the Empire's money to buy powerful positions in Honorius' court. And they paid no taxes on their ill-gotten personal fortunes, while the Roman people were burdened by overtaxation.

Disgusted by what he saw in the imperial palace, Attila vowed never to allow corruption among the Huns. There would be no abuse of tribal booty by avaricious chieftains. As king of Huns, he would set an example for his ministers and their subordinates.

True to his vow, when he became king, Attila was responsible and honest, never putting his own welfare before that of his Huns. He maintained his royal position without indulging in luxury.

Attila's palace, the finest building in Etzelnburg, occupied a prominent position but was not ostentatious like the palaces and estates of the Romans. His personal habits were modest. He refused to adorn his shoes with gold and silver as many of the Hunnic noblemen did. No precious-metal mountings decorated the bows of his saddle. No jewels were embedded in the bridle worn by his magnificent war-horse. He drank from a wooden cup and ate meat served on a wooden platter. His simple clothes were kept conspicuously clean by his personal attendants. While he did not expect his Huns to restrict themselves to his unassuming ways, he insisted that they avoid extravagance.

Attila's was a disciplined mind. He understood his people's passions, fears, lust for booty, and need for victory on the battlefield. With these traits in mind, he instructed his ministers, nobles, chieftains, and warriors in self-restraint and professional leadership. The power of office was never to be abused. Tolerance for the misappropriation of funds was forbidden. Leaders must never prosper at the expense of the Huns. Attila insisted that his people must be better off than if they lived under corrupt Roman rule.

The king of Huns knew full well that his chieftains liked to wear expensive clothing and jewelry and to live in luxury. He also knew that such display affronts the less fortunate. He spoke to his chieftains and warriors about their responsibility to the Huns when spending the tribe's booty.

Attila on:
"It's Easy to Be Generous with the Huns' Booty"

I have called all you chieftains and warriors here this night to speak with you regarding the use of tribal booty. You all know that many Roman officials are guilty of felonious profit making from their office. We Huns desire none of this in our tribes.

You are leaders in whom I place tremendous trust. This trust extends to all aspects of your office, especially those wherein the temptations of personal profit lie. You are powerful role models for our warriors and Huns. Everything you do or fail to do influences them. The Huns depend on you, too, and rightfully expect you to act with integrity. Integrity precludes illicit diversion of tribal booty into your own cache.

As you are my tribal leaders, it is my obligation to provide you with all the booty you rightfully earn in the performance of your duties, and I do so. But I know that tribal leaders can misuse booty. Listen now as I give you further counsel on managing the tribe's resources.

• Power changes leaders. Some chieftains unscrupulously pursue their own financial interests and ignore the rules. They even strive to remove rules that forbid their stuffing their pockets with the Huns' booty.

• One of the most insidious ways to abuse power and position is to spend tribal monies irresponsibly.

• Chieftains are never to spend the tribe's booty in pursuits that are without value for the tribe, no matter how excellent they believe the cause.

• Chieftains who find no joy in leading their tribes work solely for booty. Not only are these weak leaders of Huns, but they are also hostages of their own greed.

• A wise chieftain reserves some of the booty from rich victories to sustain the tribe during times when booty is less abundant.

• Chieftains allocate booty according to a warrior's or Hun's contribution to victory. Contribution to victory is judged without reference to a warrior's or Hun's age, sex, race, or color.

• Chieftains who meet their own needs first—at the expense of the tribe—are worthless leaders.

• Warriors and Huns who know how to fight but expect to receive the booty of battle without engaging the enemy are weak warriors and Huns.

• Nothing angers the Huns more than a chieftain or warrior who takes the booty of battle without having earned it.

• Warriors and Huns who fight competently deserve their share of the booty of battle, and their chieftain makes sure they get it.

• In the Hunnic nation, chieftains and warriors responsible for tribal booty are not to use it for personal gain. This principle applies in all situations without exception.

• Huns work best when they are certain their efforts will be rewarded fairly.

• Winning chieftains employ only those resources necessary to achieve their goals. Conservation is a cardinal rule for leaders of robust tribes.

And now I conclude my thoughts on booty with one last bit of advice:

• Enlightened chieftains never acquire more warriors and Huns than they can afford to feed. The same goes for horses. And enlightened chieftains never accumulate more tools or weapons than their warriors and Huns can properly use and maintain.

While I discourage chieftains from being extravagant with their own booty, they are, nevertheless, free to use it as they see fit. On the other hand, I shall not tolerate wastefulness with tribal booty. To that end, chieftains are never to use our money as if it were their own. As you depart my camp, go with the understanding that I trust you to be prudent in matters of booty for those tribes you lead. See my stewards as you leave so they can provide you with food and drink for your journey. Farewell until we meet again.

IV

Warriors
Become Targets

"Dodging Arrows"

The demise of Roman leadership was well under way long before Attila rose to become king of Huns. In 293, the emperor Diocletian created a tetrarchy of joint emperors because of the military necessity of protecting the Empire's frontier. This division of responsibility also served to protect Diocletian against military usurpers. Each of the four joint rulers selected a strategically located city within the geographical area of his authority from which to supervise both military and civil matters for the Empire. Maximian, who reigned over Raetia, Italy, North Africa, and Spain, chose Milan as the location of his headquarters; in 305, this choice resulted in Milan's replacing Rome as the administrative capital of the West. Later, Visigoth attacks on Milan proved it to be too vulnerable to barbarian invasions from the north for a royal city, and in 402, Ravenna became the new imperial city of the Western Empire.

Ravenna was the home port of one of the imperial fleets, which offered ample protection along the city's Adriatic border. Numerous marshes and lagoons as well as tributaries of the Po River also provided natural defensive barriers. These watery obstacles were augmented by canals within and fortifications around the city. The only land approach into Ravenna was across a raised causeway that was easy to defend against marauding barbarian tribes.

The relocation of Honorius' court from Milan brought to Ravenna a vigorous cultural and social life—and a sharp rise in visitors. Circus races were popular. Citizens enjoyed the rewards of both trade and intellectual pursuits. Ravenna became a center for the Christian religion, and its many churches were adorned with exquisite mosaics and delicate carvings. A bustling maritime city, Ravenna had narrow cobblestone streets through which wooden-wheeled carts rumbled. Both merchants and shoppers kept up a boisterous din. Wine shops enjoyed an especially brisk business because Ravenna's water was polluted. In sum, Ravenna was an exciting and somewhat difficult city. On August 22, 408, Ravenna became the setting for a reprehensible act of treachery—the assassination of the most distinguished and powerful warrior-general to serve in the fifth-century Roman army.

To rise through the ranks of the Roman army was ordinarily a slow process, but not for Flavius Stilicho. A Vandal by birth, Stilicho had joined the Roman army because his father had served in it as a cavalry officer. Since the days of Constantine, all physically fit sons of veterans were required to enter military service.

One of the few facts recorded about Stilicho's early army life is that Theodosius the Great took an interest in his career almost immediately. Soon after appointing him to serve on an important embassy to King Shapur III of Persia, Theodosius betrothed Serena, his favorite niece and adopted daughter, to Stilicho. The Emperor's new son-in-law's first significant command was as count of the sacred stables. Greater responsibility followed when Stilicho was appointed count of domestics. Around 393, Theodosius promoted Stilicho to master of soldiers and made him the ranking military officer in the Empire, a position he fulfilled honorably for the rest of his life. That Theodosius held Stilicho in high regard was all too obvious—and after the emperor's death it led to Stilicho's brutal murder.

Although Theodosius had successfully united the Eastern and Western Roman Empires, he exercised an important right as emperor in 394, shortly before his death: He proclaimed his eldest son, Arcadius, Augustus of the East, and another son, Honorius, Augustus of the West. And so Theodosius (for reasons that are unclear now) once again divided the Empire. Perhaps he thought neither son had the maturity and wisdom to effectively rule a united empire. And perhaps he recognized that neither would ever be capable of keeping East and West united. In any event, Theodosius also appointed guardians over the young Augusti. Rufinus of Aquitaine, praetorian prefect of the East, was charged with Arcadius; Stilicho, master of soldiers and the Empire's best general, was appointed guardian over the child emperor Honorius.

The proclamation published when Theodosius died gave Stilicho total military and civic authority in the West. As master of soldiers and guardian of Honorius, Stilicho now commanded the largest and best part of Theodosius' army. Stilicho was in fact the most powerful and influential figure in either half of the once again divided Roman Empire. In the East, Arcadius did not trust Rufinus, who had no military authority, and the young emperor did not look to him for guidance. Further destabilizing the situation was the hatred between Stilicho and Rufinus, which had grown out of an earlier disagreement over the treatment of some barbarian invaders.

As son-in-law of the late Theodosius, Stilicho benefited from special opportunities and privileges not customarily available to a barbarian warrior in the service of the Roman army. One privilege, however, was denied him: succession to the throne.

A new emperor could either be appointed by the reigning emperor or be elected by high-ranking military officers. Under Roman law, these elections could be held at any time. An emperor needed, therefore, loyal generals to protect him from a challenger who could win such an election.

Stilicho might have successfully bent the law and been elected emperor, but he saw himself as ineligible because he was a Vandal—a barbarian. Stilicho took another tack and arranged for his daughter Maria to marry his young charge, Honorius. In the few brief years before Maria died, their marriage produced no male offspring. Stilicho then arranged for Honorius to marry Thermantia, another of his daughters. His efforts to secure the throne for one of his heirs did not end there. He also positioned his son, Eucherius, as a possible successor to the emperor in the Eastern Empire. Stilicho's enemies became determined to keep his heirs off the throne, and Rufinus began to build a case against him. In the years that followed, others would continue this maliciousness.

Meanwhile, Stilicho put down several barbarian uprisings and secured the aid of friendly barbarian tribes in defending the Empire. He arranged tribute to the Visigoths and so defused their threat to the Empire. His victory against the Goths at Pollentia, however, was incomplete. And he failed to pursue and destroy Alaric and his army in 403, near Verona. At Fiesole, however, he routed Radagaisus' army and gained such praise from the Romans that they erected a triumphal arch in Rome in his honor. His military record was outstanding, but not unblemished. Eventually, the case Rufinus built against Stilicho created an atmosphere in the Eastern court that encouraged treachery against the Western general.

A Greek-born palace official, Olympius, spread a malicious rumor that Stilicho planned to kill the emperor *Theodosius II* and put his own son on the throne. The rumor led to a military revolt during which soldiers killed generals, high officials, and the praetorian prefects of Italy and Gaul —all supporters of Stilicho.

As soon as the news of this revolt and the attendant massacre reached Stilicho at Bologna, his generals urged him to begin a civil war. When he demurred, they murdered his Hun bodyguards. Stilicho escaped to Ravenna, where he discovered that Honorius had issued an order for his arrest.

Stilicho was hunted down in the church where he had taken refuge and was dragged into the street by palace soldiers, who murdered and beheaded him—an ignoble end to the life of a great and loyal warrior who routinely risked his life for his emperor.

As a young hostage in the court at Ravenna, Attila had heard Stilicho's sad story. The future king of Huns was sickened by the cunning schemes devised by corrupt officials to neutralize or destroy not just Stilicho, but anyone they considered a threat. He was also disgusted by the activities of advisors and ministers who blamed their mistakes on vulnerable attendants to the court. And so it was that upon becoming king of Huns, Attila recognized how easily his own court could become corrupt and took preventative action.

Attila on:
"Dodging Arrows"

I have called this gathering of chieftains and warriors to counsel you on the unavoidable perils of success. I learned much of what I will tell you while I was a hostage in Ravenna. There, the success of many great leaders was contaminated by the corruption of scheming bureaucrats. Stilicho is an example.

Stilicho was one of the greatest generals ever to command the Roman armies. But he was so ambitious that he was perceived as a menace by rivals jealous of his accomplishments and appalled that a barbarian was master of soldiers. It shouldn't surprise you that Stilicho was brought down by these enemies and, as a result of their scheming, was put to death by Honorius, the inept emperor he had loyally served. While the corrupt Romans do not feel obliged to outsiders such as Stilicho, we Huns recognize and reward good leadership and successful performance wherever we find them.

We choose our leaders from among our most able chieftains and warriors. To be a leader of Huns, one need not be born a Hun. By the same token, a born Hun may inherit riches but is not automatically entitled to lead. Leading is an honor accessible to all, but leadership positions are granted only to those who earn them.

Like a Roman, a Hunnic leader is a potential target. The arrows shot at the backs of successful warriors and chieftains are arrows of envy, jealousy, and fear. Fear is the most dangerous. Rivals fear that a chieftain or warrior will grow too strong in power and prestige. At the same time, they fear that their own efforts will be revealed as incompetent by comparison. Be aware of both chieftains and warriors who are ruthless in their pursuit of power or who are easily swayed by schemers.

While I, Attila, king of Huns, do not want chieftains or warriors to be victims of their own success, the possibility endangers all who excel. You chieftains and warriors who meet with me tonight are all accomplished Huns. You will do well to listen carefully to my thoughts on dodging political arrows.

• Beware of chieftains who either *take* or fail to *give* credit for their subordinates' accomplishments. Such chieftains are quick to find a scapegoat when they make even a minor mistake.

• No warrior or Hun should ever be expected to take an arrow for the misdeeds or mistakes of his or her chieftain. Only a dumb warrior or Hun and a cowardly chieftain engage in such an arrangement.

• An accomplished warrior's worst political enemies are colleagues who see her or his strength as a sign of their own weakness.

• To attract political enemies, warriors don't have to be good at everything. They just have to excel at whatever threatens their colleagues' security.

• As your reputation is the first target of a political opponent's arrows, never say or do anything you don't want remembered.

• Warriors are advised never to threaten the authority of self-doubting, dictatorial chieftains.

• Candidly disclosing your feelings and opinions to anyone you can't implicitly trust places political ammunition in the hands of one who may use it against you.

• Taking an arrow for a chieftain, with or without the chieftain's knowledge, tarnishes your reputation and limits your potential. Moreover, it reinforces the corruption of any chieftain who condones such a self-destructive gesture.

• A warrior with high potential is quick to leave a poorly led tribe.

• Chieftains who insist that subordinates never disagree with them lead stagnant tribes and alienate able warriors.

• Beware of the chieftain who is only pleasant and complimentary toward you in the company of others. Treacherous chieftains always appear to be friendly with those they seek to bring down, until the moment they kill them.

• The best chieftain a warrior can fight for is the one who accepts both accountability and responsibility for the duties of office—and expects the same from all subordinates.

• Warriors avoid unnecessary problems by not assuming unwarranted authority.

• Acting on dumb decisions doesn't improve them. Competent warriors avoid acting on a chieftain's dumb decisions, because following through only makes matters worse.

And I now bring this gathering to an end with this thought:

• The best Hunnic chieftains and warriors focus on dominating the Romans instead of on inciting internal division and civil war.

As I have told you before, success makes you a target. While I don't have any problem with the Romans' shooting each other in the back with political arrows, I will not indulge any warrior or chieftain among the Huns who schemes against one of our own. But my desires alone cannot curtail political infighting. Unless we work together, such infighting will weaken our tribes and nation. As I bid you farewell, I admonish you to be models of political integrity that all Huns can emulate.

V

Reality

"Practical Dreaming"

Sometime near 414 Attila was released from the court of Honorius. Had he believed the opinion prevailing among the Romans, Attila would have succumbed to the notion that the Huns' only potential was as auxiliary cavalry for the Empire's army or as field slaves.

Although Huns were primitive in appearance, customs, and manners, the young Hunnic prince was too self-assured to be influenced by others' views of what is possible. He had the courage to dream of the best the Huns could become. They were an emerging people; their place in society was not yet fixed. A sparse nomadic existence represented their past and present but not their future. They had a great destiny to realize through unity of purpose and common goals. Not for long would the Empire enlist Hunnic warriors as mercenaries to fight for a nation whose prosperity they could never share.

Attila had a marvelous capacity for conceiving grand plans, and he was fully schooled in the Empire's strengths and weaknesses. He knew that its rulers were ineffectual, its officials corrupt, and its people only too willing to let foreigners defend them while they pursued the rewards of private enterprise. He also recognized that tribal leaders had to stop competing with each other and start pooling their creativity, energy, and resources in order to create opportunity for their children and grandchildren. He envisioned the Huns building cities and becoming successful traders, manufacturers, farmers, and rulers of the world. He resolved, therefore, to lead the Hunnic army in a Great Conquest of the world.

Attila believed nothing is impossible. But to become successful as a nation, the Huns first had to heal any division among them. Their leaders had to win the loyalty of rebels and grumblers. Attila's Great Conquest would require discipline, and Hunnic chieftains had a natural arrogance and independence that must be focused on national goals. Using his skill as a master diplomat, Attila insisted that cross-purposes would no longer be tolerated, and problems should be resolved quickly. At the same time, mutual respect and trust must be established. War should be avoided as long as the Huns could achieve their goals through diplomacy. Whenever battle became inevitable, however, the Huns should employ adroit strategies and precise tactics to minimize risk. Yet war must be fought without restraint and, indeed, with enough cruelty and viciousness to discourage future enemies and to ensure a Hunnic victory.

Attila knew that to realize his plan for the Hunnic nation would take time. He and his supporters would face obstacles, conflicts, and the criticism of nobles and tribal chieftains who did not believe they could change their world for the better. Nonetheless, Attila's faith in the Huns was such that he knew they could turn the course of history. His duty was to lead them from failure to success, from resignation to renewal. Only he, with his first-rate mind, his patience, and his willingness to endure adversity, could guide the Huns to a level where they could enjoy life's richest pleasures. Since his work was too great to accomplish alone, he solicited the support of tribal chieftains camped from the Danube to the Great Wall of China. During his travels, he promoted his vision of the Huns' future. And so he forged the Hunnic confederacy, which rose to challenge the dominance of Roman rule in the fifth century.

As in any organization, Attila had to periodically reiterate the long-term vision. He knew what the Huns could achieve working together, and he wanted his plan for the Great Conquest to survive his own death. As an elder, therefore, he took advantage of having his sons gathered to celebrate his May–December marriage and counseled them on their responsibility to continue the work that he had begun.

Attila on:
"Practical Dreaming"

My sons, I have asked you to join me here on the eve of my wedding feast to the beautiful Ildico. Over the past few months, you have become impatient with your father for not granting you your promised kingdoms. I have vowed that to you, Denghizik, will go China; to you, Emnedzar, Gaul; to you, Uzindar, Italy; to you, Ernak, Persia; and to you, Geisen, Africa. Waiting to claim these lands, you all have grown increasingly jealous of your elder brother, Ellak, whom I have already made sovereign over the Acatzires— where he remains this night. You are anxious and ambitious to become rulers too. Although you have expertly commanded your units of our Hunnic cavalry, you are not yet prepared to reign over your own provinces. You have much to learn, as does your brother Ellak, although he rules the Acatzires well. Like you, he lacks the knowledge and wisdom required of a king over Hunland. We gather here tonight for your instruction, because when I die, one of my sons will take my place as king. I regret that Ellak cannot be here too.

I grow old. My mind is strong, but my body lacks the vigor to sustain me until we achieve our Great Conquest. I envisioned our new world long ago. My father, King Mundzuk, never schooled me in impossibilities, so the only fear I had was that the Huns might remain the slaves of foreigners and never earn an honorable place in history.

We have made great progress. Of course our nation still

has sporadic problems with rebel chieftains, but I have shown you how to restore order when it is challenged. Some of our Hunnic nobles have tried only to discourage your efforts. They were satisfied with too little and were immune to possibility. They scoffed at my dream of a better world. I have proved them wrong. We have established not only permanent villages but also our capital city, Etzelnburg. Our people suffer less from exposure to the elements than before. Hunting and gathering are no longer our only sources of food. And most important of all—we have escaped bondage to the Romans. Nevertheless, much remains to be done.

Another campaign awaits us in just a few short days. Aëtius—once our friend and tribal blood brother—is now a superior battlefield commander for the Romans. We know this because his army chased us from the Catalaunian Fields. Aëtius is planning to join his troops with those of a new enemy—the emperor Marcian. Remember that not only did Marcian succeed Theodosius as emperor of the Eastern Roman Empire, but also he is a seasoned commander. The combined forces of Aëtius and Marcian will not be easily defeated.

I pledge to lead you in what will be my last journey into war. Future campaigns will be yours to lead in order to secure your own provinces. Do not become hasty or self-serving. The work you do to fulfill the dreams, hopes, and goals of our nation of Huns must be pursued without personal ambition. Remember always that our Great Conquest is too grand a design to abandon. It will take longer to accomplish than I expected, but our nation must continue to be ruled by one who can lead the Huns toward this common goal. I am undecided about which of you will succeed me as king, so I will now share with all of you here my wisdom on the topic of holding fast to our ideals and objectives as a nation of Huns. As we gather strength for another great battle, it is wise to pause and reflect.

- A plan for the future is a North Star to nation and tribe.

- Chieftains who lead their tribes to victory have shared their goals with their warriors and Huns.

- A chieftain who doesn't plan for him- or herself is always reacting to the plans of others. You lose if reaction becomes your only option.

- Ordinary Huns accept fate (whatever life deals them) as their destiny. Warriors use their fate to create their destiny.

- Stamina, will, courage, and self-confidence distinguish winners from losers. Chieftains are expected to develop these attributes in their warriors and Huns.

- A chieftain doesn't waste time by trying to learn more lessons from an experience than it contains.

- Huns who interfere with the goals and ambitions of their tribe serve the Romans.

- Huns readily follow a chieftain who improves the quality of their lives; there is no compelling reason to follow one who doesn't.

- Huns never abandon a cause as long as it enhances their own lives. Warriors actually pursue causes that add value to their own lives. The best chieftains, however, support causes that improve the lives of warriors and Huns.

- Chieftains accomplish greater feats when they focus their warriors and Huns on tribal rather than individual goals.

- Frequently, unpredictable and uncontrollable external factors derail a chieftain's plan of action. As a result, adaptability to circumstance is vital to a chieftain's success.

- Chieftains, warriors, or Huns are never more disappointed in themselves than when they have had a chance to achieve more but settled for less.

- Warriors and Huns are never more disappointed in their chieftain than when she or he has promised much but delivered little.

- The most successful chieftains are realistic and pragmatic. Denial, self-deceit, and negative thinking are ultimately fatal for chieftains and their followers.

- It is better for a Hun to attempt many things and fail at a few of them than to attempt few things and fail at most of them.

- A winning chieftain can spot the opportunity to win in any form.

- Dreaming great dreams is more practical than engaging in small, unproductive activities.

- A chieftain's strategies must be as practical and workable as they are imaginative. A healthy imagination is the hallmark of a good chieftain.

And now I conclude my counsel with one last thought:

- A chieftain's greatest reward lies in helping the Huns prosper. Enjoying the personal prosperity a chieftain acquires is only a secondary pleasure.

These words of instruction will serve you well as you lead our tribes and nation in the future. For now, let us enjoy the festivities of my wedding, and in a few days, we will lead our armies to win the battles that await us. Then our nation once again will enjoy the fruits of victory and take another step in achieving our great destiny.

VI

A Position
of Strength

"Cultivating Allies"

The Roman Empire's policy of peace, established and secured by the Empire's superior military forces, was a gift to all its citizens and subjects. From time to time, its formidable army was reorganized by the emperor in order to reduce the risk of internal revolts. Ambitious generals were thus prevented from staging coups. Garrison forces were stationed in well-fortified, permanent military camps along the frontiers. Expeditionary forces were stationed in other strategic locations, from which they could respond to military threats to the Empire. The emperor himself was protected by elite palace guards.

Without question, the Romans were masters of war who gave neither mercy nor quarter to barbarian invaders. The Roman army pillaged the villages it conquered and settled Roman farmers on acquired lands. When the Romans banished or executed tribal chieftains, barbarian women of the defeated tribes often killed their own children and then committed suicide to avoid becoming prisoners of the ferocious Romans.

The imperial Roman army, for the most part, was led by Roman generals who commanded Roman warriors so skilled that they seemed to be at one with their weapons. Army materiel included superior individual weapons and armament along with crew-served war machines. Army tactics were eclectic, borrowed from, among others, the Carthaginians, Macedonians, and Spanish. The army of the

Roman Empire was, in short, so effective a war-fighting machine that it remained unequaled for hundreds of years (approximately 30 B.C. to A.D. 215). Then in 378, the warrior-chieftain Fritigern and his Visigoths trounced Emperor Valens and his forces at the Battle of Adrianople—and ended forever the unquestioned military might of the Empire.

By the turn of the fifth century, many of the Empire's finest generals and warriors had been killed in battle, and the once great Roman army began precipitously to disintegrate. Civil wars brought the best units back from the frontiers to defend the throne from usurpers. A decline in the birthrate and an increase in the demand for Roman peasants to do the work once performed by slaves created a shortage of recruits. As a result, the emperor established estates for barbarian tribes on abandoned lands within Roman borders, then depended on these barbarians to protect the frontiers. The Romans' defeat at Adrianople had taught them the importance of a cavalry to counter invading barbarians, but Romans were ineffective as horse warriors and had to hire barbarian mercenaries as cavalrymen. In other words, because the Roman Empire had no allies, it had to rely on barbarian mercenaries to augment its once autonomous army in protecting the Empire.

By the time Attila threatened the Empire, the Roman army was led by Germanic warrior-generals who were less likely to stage a coup than were the earlier Latin generals. The Roman people were now quite indifferent to the campaigns of their army, because their native sons had been replaced in military service by allied barbarians—Visigoths, Vandals, Iberians, Scandinavians, Slavs, and Asiatics. The Romans were free to pursue commerce and trade, which is where they focused their attention. Self-interest replaced interest in the Empire's well-being.

By the middle of the fifth century, the principal threat to the peace and security of both halves of the Roman Empire came from the restless and relentless Huns, who were ready to launch their Great Conquest. Their king, Attila, was an extraordinary judge of character who did not restrict the honor of leadership to Huns. Although it is unlikely that the Huns themselves were delighted by the presence of foreigners in their camp, they respected Attila's ability to marshal talent without respect to national origin. After all, he had spent over a quarter of a century developing allied relationships with any tribe or nation that would further the Huns' cause. They also knew he was not whimsical in making appointments. He selected the most able candidates to be ministers and military leaders. These included Africans, Celts, Greeks, Germans, Persians, Spaniards, and even Romans. Among the Romans were gifted soldiers of fortune, disaffected officials, secretaries, and interpreters tired of monotonous routine in the Empire. Mercenaries employed by Attila were drawn to a life of danger and the promise of enormous booty. Some newcomers brought families with them. Others intermarried after they arrived. The diversity of his followers did not mask the presence of spies, who were sent by the Empire to his camp. He, in turn, infiltrated both the Western and Eastern Empires with spies of his own.

Under Attila, the Huns' strongest allies included the Gepids, the Ostrogoths, and, ostensibly, the Vandals. At the peak of its might, Attila's confederacy was a source of serious concern at both Ravenna and Constantinople.

Attila was a skilled diplomat able to align other tribes with the Hunnic nation. He also perceived the value of having personal allies within his own tribes. Because allies leverage a leader's peacetime influence and battlefield potency, the king of Huns met with his chieftains and counseled them on the power derived from forming coalitions and eliciting personal loyalty.

Attila on:
"Cultivating Allies"

When I resolved to turn the tides of history and lead the Huns to a Great Conquest of the world, I knew that my plan required not only all the Hunnic tribes under the rule of one king but also the Ostrogoths, Gepids, and Bagaudae as allies.

I now hope to make allies out of the Franks, the Visigoths, and all the Slavic tribes as well. But should I fail to convince them that a coalition with the Huns is good for them, I will try to persuade them not to align with the Romans.

Personal alliances are as important as alliances with other nations. When I was a child, I was a hostage in the imperial court at Ravenna. I observed there the treachery Honorius faced from his own ministers and advisors. Enervating conflicts and deadly confrontations made cooperation impossible and weakened his administration. To avoid similar subversion within my own council, I sought strong chieftains and warriors—like Onegesius, Scotta, and Edecon—who enthusiastically joined my cause. As my personal allies, they have made enormous contributions to the success our nation of Huns enjoys. With them, I have accomplished much more than I ever could have without them.

All allies are important to leaders. The help of other tribes and nations is key to the defeat of formidable foes. The help of strong warriors makes strong chieftains possible.

To support you in forming alliances both inside and outside your tribes, I have these thoughts for you to consider.

• Wise chieftains will not march into battle against a clearly superior foe without first strengthening their own forces with those of an ally.

• The finest warriors are fearless in choosing sides. Wise chieftains, therefore, convince them to choose their side.

• When a powerful potential ally refuses to support you, give that ally good reasons for not supporting your enemy either.

• When highly successful warriors choose which relationships to cultivate, they woo the gatekeepers (even incompetent ones) and thereby gain access to decision makers.

• The most successful warriors win the allegiance of the decision makers.

• Chieftains must know when, where, and with whom to take sides. Therefore, they should keep fully apprised of activities within their own nation—and within the enemy's nation.

• Chieftains who plan to fight great battles in the future do well to maintain diplomatic ties with current enemies, because today's foes can become tomorrow's comrades-in-arms.

• When developing allies, do not meddle in their affairs that are of no concern to your relationship.

• All who desire to become great chieftains know that real heroes have both brain and brawn. Only the shrewdest among these, however, realize that heroes always use their brain before engaging their brawn. It follows that making allies of your foes is better than fighting them, and diplomacy is better than war.

• Because an ignored ally becomes indifferent or hostile, the best chieftains nourish even well-established relationships.

• All chieftains, however bright, need healthy alliances with members of their own tribe and with chieftains of other significant tribes.

• Accomplished leaders make a point of disturbing the status quo. Few actions are more disruptive to your opposition than your making an ally of a formerly neutral party.

• Opportunities for turning enemies into allies are ephemeral. Chieftains are sensitive to such moments and take advantage of them.

• A threat to the confederacy galvanizes the Hunnic nation. A threat to the camp galvanizes the tribe. Both threats strengthen the bonds among comrades.

• The best chieftains, understanding the thin line between fear and hatred, reject fear as an acceptable motivator of nations, tribes, or individuals—for fear can quickly turn into hatred.

And one final thought on cultivating allies:

• Uncommitted warriors or Huns are vulnerable to enticing ideas—good or bad—so their patriotism is marginal. A chieftain wins his or her warriors' and Huns' loyalty before asking them to fight for the tribe or nation.

No chieftain can win without the assistance of his or her warriors and Huns. Likewise, to endure against the vicissitudes of unforeseen obstacles, nations too must have allies. Now, the smell of the roasting boar tells me that it is time to eat.

VII

Doing Battle

"The Inevitability of Confrontation"

During the years when Attila was forming his confederacy of Huns, the greatest challenge to the Western Roman Empire was to endure internal wars. An organization's worst enemies are seldom external. Rather, the most deadly and damaging threats come from those who are so driven toward power that their political maneuvering can destroy the very group in which they seek authority. Power-hungry people distract colleagues from their duties, use institutional resources to gain personal power, and very often create dire outcomes for themselves as well as for innocent bystanders. And so it was even in the early fifth century.

The Eastern Roman Empire enjoyed cultural solidarity. Its provinces were economically viable and its military was strong. The emperor of the East kept his generals in check by dividing supreme military authority among several masters of soldiers. As a consequence, the East was often petitioned by the West for support.

In the Western Roman Empire, frontiers were constantly being invaded by various barbarian tribes. The Italian peninsula depended heavily on Africa for grain, a circumstance that would prove costly. And attending to its own needs first, the landed class refused to allow the army to raise recruits from among its agricultural labor force. Instead, landowners made payments to the Senate, which reluctantly hired barbarian mercenaries—often led by their own chieftains. These barbarians had no military tradition of the tight organization and strict discipline that were essential to meeting the Empire's military needs. The West had been further weakened by the battlefield loss of many of its most adept commanders.

In an attempt to respond swiftly to barbarian threats, the Western Command stationed troops at numerous small garrisons along the Empire's vast frontier. This decentralization deprived the West of the ability to mobilize a massive fighting force should the need arise. Decentralization required many generals, and each general had a full command staff. The result was typical of poorly executed decentralization: too many officers and, as a result, escalation of operational costs. The economic burden plus the wasteful spending of bureaucrats put a precipitous drain on Ravenna's treasury.

The army had never before been so separated by distance and divided by mission. Long campaigns far from home, a rugged life, and low pay created discontent and, even with mercenaries, a shortage of manpower. The traditions, discipline, and leadership of even the few remaining traditional Roman army troops began to break down. Under capable leadership, all these problems could have been reversed, but a reversal of the West's military problems was not to be. One reason was that although the West had several masters of soldiers, one of them was appointed as supreme military commander and prime minister—a position that contained more power than the position of emperor itself.

At his death, Theodosius the Great had left a reasonably strong army in the Eastern Empire and a stronger army in the Western Empire. In the West, however, the army came apart when three masters of soldiers—Felix, Boniface, and Aëtius—launched a bitter contest for the office of supreme military commander and prime minister in the West.

Felix was a talented general who cultivated a pious image, although he is credited with committing terrible crimes against the church. He was single-minded in his efforts to gain secular position and power.

Boniface was well known for his military skill. When the general he had followed omitted him from the roster of those that marched into Spain against the Vandals, Boniface sought revenge by taking over territory in Africa, where he became count and governed on behalf of the West.

Aëtius was the son of a military officer who had lost his life during a revolt of his troops, which had probably been instigated by Alaric the Visigoth, a powerful rival. As a child, Aëtius was held hostage first by Alaric and the Visigoths, then later by Rugila and the Huns. Although a hostage, Aëtius was treated well by the Huns and learned to get along with them. His experiences as a hostage ultimately proved to be of great consequence when Aëtius allied his forces first with the Huns against the Visigoths and later with the Visigoths against the Huns.

The fighting among these three military commanders occurred during a period of turmoil that weakened the rule of the Theodosian family in Ravenna. After Honorius died, Theodosius II (emperor of the East) named the child Valentinian III Western emperor and sent him and his mother, Placidia (who was Honorius' half-sister), to Ravenna. An army accompanied them because, upon the death of Honorius, the throne had been usurped by Johannes, a Roman nobleman (commonly referred to as John the Usurper). Castinus became the supreme military commander in the West under Johannes.

In a demonstration of his support for Valentinian and the legitimate dynasty, Boniface blockaded shipments of grain out of Africa to Rome. The people of Italy depended on Africa's grain, so Johannes dispatched Felix to break the blockade. Felix not only took a considerable army with him, leaving Ravenna without protection from Valentinian's approaching army, but also failed to break the blockade.

Having no internal resources to draw on, Johannes sent Aëtius to raise an army of Huns to prevent Valentinian and Placidia from reaching Ravenna. The Huns were quick to accept the gold Aëtius offered for their services. But Aëtius and his Hunnic army arrived at Ravenna three days too late. The capital had been taken by the army accompanying little Valentinian and his mother, Placidia. Johannes had been executed and Castinus had been removed as master of soldiers in the West.

Holding the reins of power for her son, Placidia was dismayed by the presence of an ambitious and hostile military commander like Aëtius and his sixty thousand Huns, so she paid the barbarians to "just go home." Being the entrepreneurs they were, the Huns took the gold and left.

Placidia was now calling the shots for the Western Empire because Valentinian was only six or seven years old. She needed a master of soldiers of the West in place fast. Felix was her first choice. He had convinced her that he was loyal to the new government and was senior in rank to Aëtius.

Meanwhile Aëtius, appointed as master of soldiers in Gaul, had grown in power and influence through his decisive victories there. Felix saw Aëtius as a threat to his own influence in the West and decided to murder him. But Aëtius discovered the plot and killed both Felix and his wife.

Placidia then designated Aëtius supreme military commander and prime minister in the West. Aëtius gained such great influence over Placidia that he eventually persuaded her to recall Boniface from Africa. Suspecting that Aëtius would kill him as he had Felix, Boniface remained in Africa, inviting the Vandal king, Gaiseric, to join him there. Boniface's alliance with the Vandals was devastating for Africa; it led to the loss of granaries and to default on the enormous revenues paid to Ravenna by Roman nobles who owned vast estates in Africa. Moreover, the Mediterranean ceased to be safe for Roman commerce and trade.

When he finally recognized the magnitude of the calamity he had caused, Boniface made peace with Placidia. She in turn sent him an army with which to regain Africa, but he failed in this mission. Nonetheless—and quite inexplicably

—Boniface recovered politically and was invited by Placidia to join her and Valentinian at Ravenna, where she appointed him supreme military commander and prime minister in 432. Aëtius, furious at being replaced by Boniface, led an army against him and lost. Boniface died shortly thereafter—some scholars say of disease, but many attribute his death to an injury sustained in battle (possibly from Aëtius' sword).

Banished to one of his estates, Aëtius soon learned that Boniface's son-in-law intended to kill him. Aëtius fled to the Huns and appealed to King Rugila to provide him with an army of fierce Hunnic warriors. Rugila agreed, but not without exacting a heavy price. Aëtius had to concede the Roman province of Pannonia Prima to the Huns and leave his son Carpilio with them to ensure that he keep his promise not to try to retake Pannonia Prima.

Aëtius returned to Ravenna with his Huns, and Placidia had little choice but to agree to restore him as master of soldiers and prime minister in the West, positions he held until his death. Aëtius kept his army of Huns with him until he had built a strong power base—whereupon he sent them home. And so it was that the conflict among the generals ended.

It was a conflict not over who would be emperor, but over who would be the supreme military and civic authority in the West, wherein the real power lay. It was an internecine battle that could have been averted had there been strong leadership on the throne. The greed and ambition of three military officers destroyed the personal fortunes of many prominent Roman families and brought unimaginable ruin to northern Africa. The rivalry caused a civil war that led to permanent loss of important Roman provinces. Unfortunately, a nation's most devastating enemies may also be those sworn to serve it, if they put their own self-interests above their country's well-being.

Attila, understanding confrontation as an inevitable aspect of leadership and achievement, met with his chieftains and warriors to tutor them in how to handle inevitable confrontations.

Attila on:
"The Inevitability of Confrontation"

As I ponder the domestic policies of the Roman Empire, I conclude that none have produced more calamity for the West than the decision to have an office that wielded more power than the emperor. The West could have learned from the East's multiplicity of masters of soldiers and separation of military and civic authority, but didn't. And as a result, three of the West's most capable generals sought to destroy each other in order to gain the ultimate military and civil power and authority in the West—de facto ruler at Ravenna. If these generals had not fought each other but instead had unified their efforts against us and other invaders, their realm would not be shrinking today. Let us learn from our adversary's woes.

Our tribes must compete in order to thrive. It is natural for strong warriors to compete against each other, and not always for power and booty. Quite often real warriors confront each other just for the thrill of competition. Only rarely do two competing Huns feel they have both won, even if each of them gains something from their encounter. What is much more common is for competing Huns to believe they cannot win unless the other loses —and badly! This error in judgment can have serious consequences.

Although confrontation and competition go hand in hand because both involve an encounter, you should understand that today's enemies are often tomorrow's allies. Just look at us Huns. Our armies have served longer as allied auxiliary forces of the Empire than as its battlefield foes. Remember, too, the Visigoths under Theodoric were long-time adversaries of the West Romans, and Aëtius used much of his army's resources fighting them. Later, the Visigoths aligned with Aëtius' forces to combat us at the Battle of Châlons on the Catalaunian Fields in Gaul.

While it is best to win, it is also good to allow your foes to survive with dignity in order to spare yourself the necessity of having to deal with them as enemies on a permanent basis. Aëtius treated me with respect at the disastrous Battle of Châlons, from which we retreated and which we, therefore, lost. Later, we showed mercy to the Romans by sparing Rome at the pleading of Pope Leo.

Confrontation is the two-edged sword of successful leadership. When our nation prospers, it becomes the target of lesser nations who want to share in our wealth. Our tribes and nation must fight even harder and more efficiently then. If other nations want to share in the wealth of our land, they have to work harder and more efficiently themselves or accept only what little we are willing to concede to them. We share only with partners whose contribution to the welfare of all is equal to ours. If they benefit from our wealth, we insist on benefiting from theirs.

The other edge of the leader's sword is competition. Robust competition is healthy because there is sufficient abundance and opportunity in the world for all nations to cooperate in satisfying their needs. But unless these needs are assessed realistically, those in power who live lives of wanton avarice will lead us into toxic competition that can be our downfall. We need cohesive competition, not divisive confrontation.

As chieftains and warriors, you are charged with control of confrontation. Encourage only healthy, productive competition in your tribes. This is not a simple matter and must be watched over with care.

You are also charged with leading your tribes against our nation's foes. Our tribes may not always win, but they must always stand ready and prepared to confront the challenges of our enemies. Listen now to my words of counsel.

• A Hun should learn early in life that not every Hun will be his or her friend. Nevertheless, a Hun who is not a friend need not be an enemy.

• Because warriors accept competition as an inevitable part of life, they look for ways to excel at it.

• Huns who compete don't always win. Huns who don't confront their fears, challengers, and foes never win.

• When attacking, chieftains exploit the enemy's weaknesses first—unless by intelligent maneuvering or brute force they can neutralize the enemy's strengths.

• Chieftains should avoid doing battle when both winning and losing will cost too much.

• Winning past battles doesn't entitle Huns to win future battles. It does, however, increase the odds that they will win future battles. Winning is as much a habit as it is an outcome.

• Chieftains do not always get along well with their warriors. Conversely, warriors do not always get along well with their chieftains. A certain level of conflict is often present between a leader and those ambitious to lead.

• Huns are quick to revolt against oppressive chieftains who treat them like slaves.

• Often the greatest advances for the Huns result from a single chieftain's courage to buck tradition by leading the tribe on the difficult, unpopular course to innovation.

• It is impossible for a Hun to be liked by every other Hun, because what is natural for one is unnatural for the other. Chieftains and warriors see such opposition for what it is—an honest difference—and do not fret about it.

• Warriors and Huns must learn that following the best-qualified chieftain is desirable but not always possible. Likewise, following the chieftain whom they most admire is desirable but not always possible. Following whoever is leader of the tribe is, however, nonnegotiable. They should, therefore, leave the tribe if they can no longer follow its leader, and join a tribe whose leader inspires their allegiance.

• Winning chieftains recognize symptoms of individual or organizational dysfunction in their tribes and fix the problem.

• Warriors or Huns who believe they know more than their chieftain are difficult to lead, resist tribal discipline, cause disruption, and are seldom worth the effort required to reform them.

• One tribe led by two chieftains can never be at top form in battle. A nation with two equal leaders invites disaster.

• Warriors and Huns who don't feel secure are difficult to lead.

• Seasoned chieftains are less concerned with whether or not their warriors and Huns approve of their orders than with whether or not these followers understand the orders. While it is good if everyone not only understands the chieftain's directions but also approves of them, it is best that anyone who frequently disapproves joins another tribe.

• Although chieftains who work hard to gain consensus for their decisions may ultimately gain agreement, they may never do the things necessary to move the tribe forward.

• Huns are not free to choose which tribal rules to follow. The same principle applies to warriors and chieftains. This, however, doesn't mean that obsolete or bad rules can't be changed.

• Chieftains whose main desire is to be liked and accepted will surely fail to achieve this goal when they must make unpopular decisions. But chieftains who won't make unpopular decisions that are clearly in the best interests of the tribe are gutless.

• A chieftain isn't paid to solve a warrior's or Hun's personal problems. Warriors or Huns who ignore this basic fact and constantly talk about their personal problems with their chieftain soon have another personal problem—no job.

• Criticizing successful Huns gives unaccomplished Huns a rare opportunity to feel important, but such backbiting undermines the morale of the competent majority.

• Nasty gossip, superfluous competition, and petty jealousy obstruct tribal effectiveness.

• Chieftains may not always gain the rewards they deserve, but they do reap whatever rewards they can negotiate.

• Wise chieftains try to resolve honest differences with their advisors before enforcing their own will.

And in closing:

• Weak chieftains, when faced with confrontation, often do the easiest thing—nothing—and so avoid risk. But when they do nothing, they contribute nothing of consequence to the tribe.

Now that I have spoken to you on the inevitability of confrontation, I charge you to go forth and apply my counsel as you lead our tribes toward the great destiny that awaits us as a nation of Huns.

VIII
Falling on Your Own Sword

"Self-inflicted Wounds Are Hazardous to Your Career"

Virtually nothing is known about his early career, but Litorius had risen to become Aëtius' chief lieutenant by the time Aëtius started his campaign to solidify control over the Western Roman Empire in Gaul. Thought by some scribes of his day to be master of soldiers in Gaul, Litorius gained a reputation as an accomplished warrior. Skilled in military strategy and tactics, he was a complex man whose actions could conflict with his own self-interest. Litorius was self-reliant to a fault, arrogant, impious, and prone to ignore the judgment of others. Because he was too ambitious, he made every attempt to eclipse Aëtius in fame.

Litorius' desire to win battles for the Empire—and thus to outshine Aëtius—was compromised by his lax control over his army as it moved from campaign to campaign. His army was primarily composed of Hunnic warriors who had been lent to Aëtius by King Rugila. Litorius' failure to keep a tight rein on his Huns was a fatal blunder.

After defeating the Bagaudae—a group of poor people, slaves, and highwaymen in northwestern Gaul—Litorius headed for Narbonne. As he led his column past the estate of the Roman general Avitus (who later became the emperor of the West), an especially vicious Hun killed one of Avitus' servants for no apparent reason. Avitus had always scorned Aëtius and Litorius for making military alliances with the Huns, so when he learned of his servant's senseless murder, he armed himself and rode with his own troops after the army of Litorius. In a single battle, Avitus took revenge for the slaying of his servant.

Despite heavy battle losses to Avitus, Litorius rode on to his assignment to end the Visigoth siege at Narbonne. Relieving Narbonne was vital to the Roman Empire's commitment to its interests in Gaul. Narbonne, the first Roman colony beyond the Alps, not only was the center of the flourishing province of Gallia Narbonenis but also was an important center of trade, strategically located near the Gulf of Lions.

Although Litorius was remiss in his discipline of his Hunnic warriors, he was no fool about preparing for Narbonne —a city nearing the point of surrender. The Visigoth siege had outlasted the city's food supply. The people of Narbonne seemed to be on the verge of either a military defeat or starvation. Aware of their predicament, Litorius procured two bushels of grain for each of his Hunnic warriors to carry to Narbonne. As they neared the city, the Huns stacked their grain, then routed the Visigoths with amazing speed. By removing the Visigoth threat and also by feeding the near-starved citizens of Narbonne, Litorius added to his stature as a hero of Gaul.

During the next two years, Litorius and his Huns battled the Visigoths successfully. Then, in 439, Litorius and his Huns laid siege to the Visigoth capital at Toulouse in southern Gaul, northwest of Narbonne. The Visigoths were demoralized by the great number of their warriors who had been killed in battles. Discouraging them further was the news that Aëtius was leading his own forces toward southern Gaul. In the preceding year alone, Aëtius' army had killed over eight thousand Visigoths.

Believing their defeat to be inevitable, the Visigoths simultaneously prayed to God for protection and sent members of the clergy to Litorius to plead for peace. The Visigoths were willing to forfeit some of their personal wealth and land to avoid loss of life and the destruction of Toulouse as well.

But Litorius believed taking Toulouse by force was essential to his career. Ignoring his advisors' recommendation to accept peace, he quickly rejected the Visigoths' pleas to spare them and their city. The opportunity to outshine his own leader, Aëtius, was too great a temptation to resist, and Litorius intensified his preparations to take the city. On the eve of his attack on Toulouse, he allowed the Huns' haruspices to perform their ancient sacrificial ceremony, as usual, to divine the outcome of the pending battle. Assured by their prophecy that he would win, Litorius then attacked the Visigoths. Initially, his Huns slew tremendous numbers of Visigoths, but the fortunes of war turned as the battle heightened. Litorius himself was captured. Without their battlefield leader, the Huns lost their fighting pizzazz and made disastrous errors. By battle's end, all the Huns serving in Litorius' army had been slain by the Visigoth defenders at Toulouse. For his part, Litorius did no better than his Hunnic warriors. He was taken into the city and executed. Litorius had made the fatal mistake of overestimating his own strength, while the Visigoths had underestimated theirs. Diplomacy could have salvaged a situation that without it ended in many deaths.

In contrast, Attila never took by force that which he could gain by diplomacy. He knew how unpredictable the balance of power is. He also understood that many of the attributes that make a warrior great can also cause his or her downfall. For instance, uncontrolled personal pride and ambition can eventually lead even great warriors to self-destruct. Aware of the dangers, Attila summoned his chieftains and best warriors to his camp for instruction on avoiding personal downfall.

Attila on:
"Self-inflicted Wounds Are
Hazardous to Your Career"

This night I have called you great chieftains and warriors to meet with me in order that I may counsel you on avoiding the pitfalls to your own success.

My uncle, King Rugila, made a pact with Aëtius to lend him an army of our Huns to help him secure Roman interests in Gaul. Aëtius placed these Huns under the command of a great general, Litorius. Our Huns who fought under Litorius were undisciplined by Roman standards. The independent spirit of our Huns must be disciplined to serve the cause. If this is not done, they will be disruptive and dangerous. Litorius should have known that discipline is essential to a strong and mighty army.

Litorius had an even greater flaw than neglect of discipline. He was ambitious, proud, and envious of his leader, Aëtius. Ambition and pride can be productive. They motivate warriors to achieve great feats. But envy is a terrible trait in a warrior. Envy drives warriors toward what another has instead of toward what is good for them personally. Envy also distracts a warrior from his or her own priorities. The results were evident in Litorius' dramatic fall at Toulouse.

As I wish no such thing to happen to any of our great chieftains and warriors, I offer these thoughts for your instruction.

• Competent leaders don't compound the obstacles that often block the road to success by making decisions that only serve to further their own personal gain.

• Leaders who keep their own counsel alone will eventually bungle important assignments and, therefore, succumb to their own incompetence. Or they will fall victim to an enemy, which is another form of incompetence. Leaders who heed the counsel of experts, who weigh the circumstances of their situation, and who consider the possible conse-quences of their actions will win more often than they lose and will avoid falling on their own swords.

• Leaders who feel secure about their position and power praise the accomplishments of others without envying them.

• Nothing is more pleasing to the warriors and Huns than the downfall of a self-important chieftain.

• While a draw is better than a loss, real leaders go for victory. And winning without having to fight, though rare, is the sweetest victory of all. Leaders are not lost to an enemy subdued through diplomacy.

• Times, weapons, tactics, and the needs of the tribe all change. The demand for competent and bold leadership persists. Leaders who desire to lead are always willing to learn—even to learn to be a better leader.

• Tough chieftains and outstanding warriors are complex people who are never fully understood by others, and some-times even they are at a loss to explain or understand their own behavior.

• Because Huns are creatures of habit, strong chieftains help them develop desirable habits—ones that won't get in their way when they're warriors.

• Warriors, beware of chieftains who are zealots. Zealots are led by their own needs even when the result may be annihi-lation of their tribe.

• When Huns find themselves with a weak leader, they be-come confused and ineffective. Huns desire to be led well.

• Without competition, warriors and Huns become com-placent and ineffective. And warriors and Huns who can't compete can't win.

- While jealousy is inevitable among chieftains, warriors, and Huns, any Hun's own personal achievement is demeaned when she or he is tormented by another's accomplishments or acquisitions.

- Huns who make a mistake only once have learned the value of experience.

- A few essential work rules increase the Huns' productivity, and productivity increases their morale. Too many rules, however, dampen both productivity and morale.

- Expertise in the service of a strong battle plan is never more important to the Huns than in their hour of crisis.

- Anyone who doesn't make mistakes isn't trying hard enough.

- Attempting to change what cannot be changed is a waste of time and resources. Distinguishing what can from what cannot be changed is fundamental to a chieftain's effectiveness.

- Asking for needed help is typical of a good Hun. Refusing needed help is typical of a stubborn Hun. The same can be said of warrior and chieftain.

- A Hun who claims to enter battle with no fear is either a moron or a liar. Morons make poor Huns, and liars soon find they are not trusted.

- Huns who believe themselves infallible become highly vulnerable to failure.

- Chieftains who give too many orders frustrate their warriors' and Huns' most outstanding efforts. Chieftains who give too few orders invite their warriors' and Huns' most mediocre efforts.

- If a chieftain values his or her regime's survival over the nation's, it's time to usher in a new regime.

- Smart chieftains never conquer and occupy any territory they can't control well into the future.

- A Hun who wants to be a warrior, or a warrior who wants to be a chieftain, increases the odds of success by concentrating on the present job, not by dreaming of the next assignment.

- Good Huns learn to solve their own problems before they become problems for other Huns or for the tribe.

- All chieftains have flaws, but substandard chieftains lack the ability to compensate for theirs.

- Huns who hold grudges live in a constant state of anxiety. Chieftains should teach these Huns how to resolve personal differences.

- Warriors and Huns who seek conflict for its own sake should be culled from the army for the good of all concerned.

- The troubles that bring anguish to a chieftain are those he or she didn't pay attention to while they were manageable.

- Chieftains should understand that the only thing worse than losing a battle is failure to learn how to win the next one.

And by way of ending our gathering, I admonish you to always keep this one last thought foremost in your mind:

- Chieftains who believe their position is secure don't comprehend the subtle risks inherent in leadership.

You chieftains and warriors must avoid falling victim to your own weaknesses. Transform your weaknesses into strengths or into former bad habits. Your tribes and our nation will always need the capable leadership and talents of great warriors. I challenge you all to be such leaders of Huns.

IX
The Test
of Character

"Equanimity in Battle"

Near the turn of the fifth century three brothers—
Mundzuk, Oktar, and Rugila—ruled the most aristocratic
Hunnic tribes. Rugila survived his brothers and became
king over their tribes as well as his own. When Rugila died,
the customary law of the Huns dictated that he should be
succeeded by his fourth brother, Aebarse, who was serving
far away from the Danube as sovereign of the Caucasian
Huns. About the same time, Theodosius II sent an embassy
to the Danube Huns. Protocol stipulated that such an embassy be met by a king. Mundzuk's sons, Attila and Bleda,
seized both opportunity and joint command of the Hunnic
throne, meeting with the Roman ambassadors as kings of
the Danube Huns. In other words, they usurped their uncle
Aebarse's throne.

Although Theodosius was emperor in the East, Aëtius,
master of soldiers and prime minister in the West, directed
Roman policy concerning the Huns. Aëtius knew only too
well the menace a united confederacy of Huns under Attila
and his brother would pose to the Empire, and he commu-
nicated this awareness to Theodosius. Acting on Aëtius' advice, Theodosius sent envoys to spread discontent among
Hunnic tribal leaders—showering them with gifts and im-
ploring them to remain independent of Attila.

Aebarse knew that his position on the Danube had been
usurped by his nephews and that Attila also planned to
bring the Caucasian Huns under his own rule. Aebarse also

knew how pugnacious Attila was and had no intention of
challenging him in battle. But he was determined to remain
king of the Caucasian Huns. Theodosius' envoys encouraged him to stand firm. On the same day that Attila learned
that Aebarse intended to rule the Caucasian Huns as an
independent nation, he also learned that the Acatzires were
about to revolt against him as the result of a payoff from the
emperor.

Attila's Great Conquest would have no chance of success
without the unification of all Hunnic tribes. In addition, all
Hunnic traitors must be punished.

Familiar with the tactics of cunning Roman diplomats,
Attila realized that both Aebarse and the Acatzires had been
bribed to reject Hunnic unification. Without decisive action
on Attila's part, rebellion would now spread and demolish
what unity he had built among the Huns during the past
twenty years. Bleda confined himself to the pleasures of
hunting and drinking. Attila, unthreatened politically by
Bleda, left him in charge of the Danube Huns and set out
for the Caucasus territories.

Attila arrived unannounced and unexpected at the camp
of his uncle Aebarse. During the many years since they had
last met, Attila had grown in power and influence. Aebarse
was now afraid of his nephew and wished that his letter
promising noninterference with Attila's and Bleda's joint
lordship over the Danube Huns had not insisted on his own
independence as king of Caucasian Huns.

Momentarily disarmed by his nephew's charming friend-
liness, Aebarse listened carefully to Attila's plan for a Great
Conquest by the Huns. It would require total loyalty of all
the tribes, including those in the Caucasus, Attila said. The
king of Huns was aware that his plan would meet some resistance from rebel chieftains. These, Attila emphasized,
would be erased from the picture. Aebarse interpreted Attila's pointed remarks as a personal message for him.

When it was Aebarse's turn to speak, the frightened king
assured his formidable nephew that he understood the

great plan for the future of the Huns. He was prepared to abandon his ambitions to remain autonomous. Attila could count on his support and on that of the tribes living in his territories. Henceforth, he would ally his tribes to Attila's Hunnic confederacy.

Diplomacy had resolved their differences without bloodshed. Accepting Aebarse's promise of loyalty, Attila added some of his uncle's warriors to his own forces, mounted his horse, and rode off across the steppes toward the land of the Acatzires.

When the Romans had paid the Acatzires in gold for their rejection of Hunnic unification, they had unwittingly offended Kuridak, a tribal noble. In retaliation, Kuridak now sent a secret courier to Attila, reporting the Acatzire alliance with the Empire.

As the Acatzires took up arms to resist the advance of Attila's approaching army, Kuridak—under the guise of a reconnaissance—led a large contingent of Acatzire warriors into the mountains. This action seriously weakened the Acatzires, and their remaining warriors were quickly and soundly defeated by Attila.

The Acatzires then realized that the Romans could not be relied on to support a rebellion they had incited. Attila took advantage of this insight and solidified his control over them. He appointed his eldest son, Ellak, as their new chieftain. Ellak would nurture their self-esteem as citizens of a Hunnic nation. And he was a chieftain in whom Attila placed complete trust.

The king of Huns understood that empathy and compassion were keys not only to forging the Huns into a nation but also to winning the hearts and minds of defeated foes. As he desired tribal leaders to understand this aspect of power, he called them to gather at his camp.

Attila on:
"Equanimity in Battle"

My uncle Aebarse, king of the Caucasian Huns, united his tribes with our Hunnic nation without my having to resort to war. This was good for all Huns. Another tribe, the Acatzires, fell victim to Roman bribes and promised the emperor's envoys that they would not join our Hunnic confederacy. This was bad for all Huns. My Great Conquest called for all Hunnic tribes to band together as one nation. Allowing one or more tribes to remain independent would not do.

Long ago, I learned that it is sometimes necessary to gain by battle that which cannot be attained by other means. And once the fighting and looting end, the battle often continues.

When we win new lands and become masters of a captive people, unless we convince them that they will gain greater rewards as our subjects than as our enemies, they will remain our enemies and resist our rule. How the conqueror treats the conquered is a test of character in war. How a chieftain treats his or her subordinates is the test of character as a tribal leader.

As there is more for you to learn about the test of character in war and as a leader, I commend these thoughts to you.

- All competent warriors are fierce in battle and merciful in victory.

- In troubled times, a chieftain who shows compassion for the Huns gains their cooperation and support.

- No warrior becomes a chieftain without having been forgiven for honest mistakes made along the way.

- Chieftains who extend common courtesy to their warriors and Huns find themselves receiving uncommon loyalty and respect in return.

- Chieftains encourage warriors and Huns to do their best but do not expect them to excel at every assignment.

- The acquisition of power changes people. All new chieftains need to learn how to employ responsibly the power and influence of high office.

- Even the worst of Huns makes fewer mistakes than a faultfinding chieftain will accuse her or him of making.

- Chieftains, warriors, and Huns do not expect to be rewarded for every accomplishment, but they expect to be criticized for every mistake.

- Chieftains should never resist helping capable, talented, and ambitious warriors to become chieftains themselves.

- In times of scarcity, Huns will work for meager booty. The same cannot be said about times of plenty.

- Chieftains often become angry with warriors or Huns who suffer from the same weaknesses that afflict the chieftains themselves.

- To be strong, our nation requires chieftains who understand the Huns' everyday lives. Chieftains who show concern for the Huns' daily problems understand that there is no other way to win their hearts.

- Chieftains can deal effectively with warriors and Huns by coupling mildness with majesty and charm with intellect in order to elicit loyalty.

- Chieftains who themselves desire admiration liberally applaud deserving warriors and Huns.

• A chieftain who praises the best aspects of his or her warriors and Huns does more to strengthen the tribe than does the chieftain who harps on minor faults.

• Chieftains who repeatedly accuse their warriors and Huns of falling short will suffer from their inadequate performances in the future.

And now I conclude our gathering with this thought:

• Every warrior and Hun has not only the right but also the obligation to improve on past performance. Chieftains must honor this right.

As you prepare to depart my camp this night, I remind you of your need to gain the trust and confidence of all your warriors and Huns. It is also important to cultivate both trust and confidence in those you conquer so that they do not remain your enemies. Be well.

Favoritism

"If You Want a Pet, Buy a Dog"

Bleda reigned with Attila as co-king of Huns for over a decade following the death of their uncle, King Rugila. Physically larger but intellectually smaller than his younger brother, Bleda had a rowdy and clamorous character that was notorious even among the Huns.

Bleda (who never fought a campaign without Attila) took a Moorish dwarf named Zerco prisoner during the capture of Sirmium in 441. He used the Moorish dwarf to amuse himself, laughing at the dwarf's stammering jumble of Latin, Hunnic, and Gothic phrases. Bleda's cruelty was so great that he even delighted in poking fun at Zerco's wrenched and painful walk. Indeed, Bleda kept the Moorish dwarf at his side during parties and took him along on subsequent campaigns—but not before his craftsmen had made Zerco a little suit of armor.

At last, Zerco was able to escape his captor with some Roman prisoners. But Bleda sent Hunnic warriors to hunt him down, then howled with raucous laughter when Zerco was brought back in chains. He asked his "little dwarf" why he wanted to escape. Wasn't he happy with life among the Huns? Zerco said it was because Bleda had never given him a wife. Bleda laughed but did arrange for Zerco to wed a Hunnic woman.

After Bleda's death, Attila sent Zerco to Aëtius in exchange for a Gallic secretary. Aëtius was no more amused by Zerco than was Attila, and the prime minister relinquished him to the Roman general Aspar. Zerco escaped to Constantinople, where the Hunnic chieftain Edecon, during his embassy there, found him. Zerco pleaded with Edecon to take him back to the Huns so he could be reunited with the wife that he had been forced to leave behind. Edecon agreed.

At a great feast celebrating the return of Edecon and Orestes to Etzelnburg, Zerco was ushered in to entertain the king of Huns and his guests. Attila regarded the dwarf's performance without amusement, put a stop to it, and did not reunite him with his Hunnic bride. What became of the little person is not known.

Attila's feelings about Bleda's mistreatment of Zerco went unrecorded, too. When Attila sent Zerco to Aëtius, his motive might have been that he saw in the little person evidence that the body cannot always be depended on—a frightening insight. Perhaps he simply believed Zerco was a fair trade for a Gallic secretary. Quite possibly, he did not want to confront daily so vivid a reminder of the dead brother he may have murdered. And he may have been disgusted at the spectacle of Zerco being treated like a pet.

One thing is certain. Attila did not condone Bleda's making a pet of Zerco. Nor did he find humor, as most others did, in exploiting deficiencies that could not be remedied. Attila would also have had zero tolerance for sycophants (people who *want* to be their leaders' pets) and would have held in contempt any leader who encouraged sycophancy. Disgusted by Bleda's treatment of Zerco, Attila counseled his chieftains and warriors on the destructive dynamics of favoritism and abuse.

Attila on:
"If You Want a Pet, Buy a Dog"

Bleda mocked all people by treating Zerco in a disgusting manner. Many of you found humor in Zerco's performances at our feasts. What you failed to consider was that

Zerco was not *acting;* he was showing us his limitations—over which he had no control. As long as I, Attila, reign as king of Huns, such mindless cruelty as was indulged in by those who laughed at Zerco will not be abided. We will treat all people, except our enemies, with dignity and appropriate compassion.

People are never to be used as pets. I have no problem with you chieftains surrounding yourselves with competent warriors and Huns whom you trust and enjoy. This is wise leadership. But I have a major objection to any chieftain either surrounding him- or herself with untrustworthy lackeys or taking advantage of a helpless subordinate.

Huns become like pets when they are protected and promoted solely because of a personal relationship with the chieftain. Huns who seek such a relationship are mocked by Huns worthy of our name. Huns who are made pets against their will should be encouraged and helped to free themselves. Moreover, it comes as no surprise that chieftains who practice favoritism lose credibility and respect.

The performance and morale of our tribes is undermined by the presence of sycophants and victims. Approval of favoritism sends the wrong message to those warriors and Huns who rightly expect to find a relationship between performance and promotion, between achievement and recognition. Warriors and Huns are to be nurtured and promoted to positions of broader responsibility on the basis of past accomplishment and perceived potential. And to that end, those chieftains who permit bootlicking or practice abuse are to be expelled from our nation. Here, then, are my words of counsel on favoritism.

• Fear motivates not only toadies and victims but also the chieftains who manipulate them. Fearing loss of authority and control, weak chieftains employ sycophant warriors and Huns who agree with their every word and obey even malevolent commands. Weak chieftains also take advantage of warriors and Huns who for various reasons cannot defend themselves.

• Weak warriors and Huns often seek to become a chieftain's pet when they lack the skill to execute their duties with the expertise typically rewarded by chieftains. Victimized warriors and Huns become a chieftain's unwilling pet when they fear that a chieftain will refuse to reward their expertise unless they allow themselves to be abused.

• Chieftains should discourage, not reward, complacency.

• Only those Huns who are mediocre are always at their best. Favoritism encourages mediocrity and discourages talent.

• Huns who unquestioningly do anything their chieftain asks of them exhibit blind loyalty. Such zealots have no place in a strong and effective tribe.

• Sage chieftains appoint their offspring or other members of their clan to leadership positions only when their warriors and Huns agree that the relative is the best-qualified person for the job. Well-qualified candidates alone are to be considered for positions of power.

• Toady Huns are an insecure chieftain's only allies, but they are easily swayed and can't be counted on when a competent Hun is needed.

• Inadequate chieftains often surround themselves with less talented warriors and Huns—or with superior warriors and Huns whom they intimidate—in order to feel more secure about their own shortcomings.

• Weak chieftains need to be number one at whatever they do, for they live in fear of losing prestige. They therefore keep company with the dull and feeble in order to outshine those around them.

• First-rate chieftains learn from disagreements with talented warriors and, therefore, encourage the challenge of their own ideas. Second-rate chieftains are quick to admonish talented warriors who disagree with them about anything.

• Huns low in potential but high in ambition are likely to suck up to their chieftain.

• Competent warriors sometimes disagree with the chieftain. When dissenting opinions are always listened to with impatience, then dismissed or evaded, the chieftain reduces his or her close circle to lackeys and incompetents.

• Chieftains who surround themselves with sycophants or victims limit their ability to improve life for the Huns and provoke rage and rebellion among conscientious warriors.

And we conclude tonight's council with this thought:

• Smart, ambitious Huns know that the best place to sharpen their abilities is in the company of able warriors. Accomplished, courageous warriors never treat their Huns like pets—nor do they allow themselves to become a chieftain's pet. Chieftains should, therefore, always assign smart Huns to accomplished warriors who will help them fully develop their talents.

You tribal leaders must set the example for others to follow. Do not misuse those who cannot defend themselves. Resist favoritism in our tribes—it discourages the competent and the brave while encouraging the incompetent and the cowardly. Be well and behave well until we meet again.

XI

Blame

"Risk-taking Can Backfire"

Edecon, a Hun, and Orestes, a Pannonian who had de-
fected to the Huns, were both trusted lieutenants of Attila.
In the spring of 449, the king of Huns dispatched them to
the emperor Theodosius II in Constantinople with a letter
explaining his dissatisfaction with the Romans' failure to
keep the terms of a peace treaty. The treaty called for the
Eastern Empire to return all Hunnic prisoners, slaves, and
deserters, and to evacuate a stretch of land south of the
Danube. Attila's letter stipulated that if Constantinople delayed any longer, he would resume the war.

In Constantinople, Edecon and Orestes were escorted by
Vigilas, one of the few attachés who spoke the Hunnic language. What he lacked in understanding of protocol, Vigilas
made up for in ambition to gain favor with the grand eunuch, Chrysaphius. Chrysaphius was sword-bearer and minister of finance, and he dominated Theodosius. An avaricious opportunist, he was busy solidifying his power.
Knowing that the real civil power in the East rested with
Chrysaphius, the Hunnic ambassadors accepted an invita-
tion to dine privately with the grand eunuch. Vigilas served
as translator during the dinner at Chrysaphius' residence,
where Edecon compared the splendor of the grand eunuch's home favorably to the Huns' more modest dwellings.
Orestes, having lived among the Romans, was less im-
pressed.

Because Chrysaphius did not trust Theodosius to respond aggressively to Attila's demands, he decided to take advantage of Edecon's naivete. Inviting him to a meeting without Orestes, he offered Edecon fifty pounds of gold to assassinate the king of Huns. Edecon appeared eager to accept the deal and asked Chrysaphius to have the gold delivered to him at Etzelnburg so he could avoid the suspicion that carrying so large a sum would provoke. The grand eunuch was delighted that his plot was so easily advanced by this simpleminded barbarian. He rushed to report the good news to Theodosius, who was skeptical and refused to believe that a trusted officer would betray the king of Huns. For once, Theodosius was more perceptive than Chrysaphius.

Edecon and Orestes returned to Etzelnburg with an embassy from Constantinople that carried a letter from Theodosius to Attila. Vigilas went along to act as interpreter, to verify that the regicide was accomplished, and to tell Edecon how the gold payment would be delivered. The head of the embassy, Maximinus, knew nothing of the secret plot to assassinate the king of Huns. Neither did Priscus, a sophist and historian who joined them on the journey. (It was during this embassy that Priscus penned the famous journal that provides interesting but curious observations about the personalities of Attila and his Huns.)

Apparently Edecon revealed the plot to his friend Orestes and immediately passed on the information to Attila on his return to Etzelnburg. The Huns then showed they were anything but naive and played the plot back against the cunning Romans with Hunnic variations.

When Attila read Theodosius' letter claiming that all demands of the peace treaty had been met, he erupted. The king of Huns ordered Vigilas to return to Constantinople with a message that if the treaty's conditions were not swiftly and fully complied with, the Huns would attack.

Playing into Attila's hands, Vigilas believed that the plot against the Hun hadn't been discovered—for if it had, would he, Vigilas, be alive to return to Constantinople with an important message?

To justify delaying the murder, Edecon told Vigilas that killing Attila was too risky an action to take alone and that the blood money must be doubled so he could hire accomplices. Vigilas returned to Constantinople and relayed this demand to Chrysaphius. The grand eunuch had hoped for better news but was desperate to rid the world of the most dreadful of all barbarians. He gave Vigilas the gold and sent him back to Etzelnburg to see to it that the job was done.

Vigilas viewed taking dirty risks for his master as necessary career moves. Chrysaphius made a dumb decision when he delegated an important assignment to a blundering opportunist. At least the eunuch was smart enough to avoid personal risk and realized that his scheme could fail. If the plot collapsed, he would blame Vigilas and even Maximinus and Priscus if necessary.

Vigilas returned to Attila in Etzelnburg, taking with him both the gold and his twenty-year-old son. (One can only guess that Vigilas was confident of his success and wanted to show the lad how things were done in the real world, for he surely wouldn't have knowingly exposed his own son to impending danger.)

Continuing to weave a web in which to catch the Roman plotters, Attila announced a new policy that prevented Roman ambassadors from purchasing anything but food while in Hunnic territories. So when Vigilas showed up with a large bag of gold, Attila asked why the Roman envoy needed so much money in a poor country where food was cheap.

Vigilas boldly replied that the money was to pay Attila ransom for Roman prisoners. Attila responded that diplomatic envoys were not allowed to purchase anything except food—not even prisoners. Then Attila asked if Vigilas was interested in buying a few horses. Vigilas said yes, the money was for a few horses. Attila roared that for a hundred pounds of gold, Vigilas could buy a whole herd of horses. And so they sparred. Was the money for furs? Yes. Livestock?

Of course. Jewels? Admittedly. By now, Vigilas was stammering. A glance at Edecon, who had just joined them, told him that Attila had uncovered the plot.

When Vigilas denied knowledge of the planned assassination, Attila demanded that the envoy's son confess. The young man insisted that he was ignorant of any plan to kill the king of Huns. Attila observed that if he was innocent, he was also superfluous and would be executed immediately. Watching Attila's bodyguards throw his son to the floor and raise their swords over his head, Vigilas cried out that the boy was innocent and that he alone was guilty. Attila replied that while he knew the boy to be innocent, he also knew Vigilas to be too dull to have devised the fatal scheme. Ordering a warrior to place his sword on the neck of Vigilas' son, Attila gave the envoy a chance to reveal who was behind the assassination plot. When Vigilas accused his master, Chrysaphius, the king of Huns was satisfied that the answer was true.

Attila wasn't after the head of Vigilas, whom he considered unimportant at best. He had Vigilas thrown into a cell; then he freed the envoy's son to return to Constantinople with Orestes, who carried a letter to Theodosius ordering the head of the grand eunuch to be sent to Attila in the very sack that had carried the ransom for the head of the king of Huns. Attila, of course, had kept the gold for his Huns.

Despite his disappointment that Chrysaphius had failed to engineer Attila's murder, Theodosius was too weak to replace the sword-bearer and finance minister with someone of real mettle. And so Theodosius agreed to comply with the terms of the peace treaty with the Huns. He also paid a ransom in more gold for Vigilas. But he drew the line at giving Attila the head of the grand eunuch, whom he depended on to run the civil affairs of the state.

In the spring of 450, shortly before his Great Conquest began, Attila met with the new embassy sent by Theodosius and agreed to revised peace terms. Then he sent Vigilas back to Constantinople with the envoys, who took gifts of

horses and furs. Vigilas carried a letter from the king of
Huns reiterating his demand for Chrysaphius' head. Outraged, Theodosius accused Vigilas of treason, blamed him
for everything that had gone wrong, and imprisoned him.
Vigilas had gambled and lost. Driven by ambition, he had
tried to impress the powerful grand eunuch by risking deep
involvement in a plot that was flawed from the outset. Vigilas now had to bear the terrible consequences of taking risks
beyond his understanding and ability. Chrysaphius, on the
other hand, was guilty but escaped all blame, just as he had
intended to do.

Attila, unlike some Roman leaders, believed that accountability is inseparable from responsibility. He taught his
chieftains and warriors, therefore, about the consequences
of risk-taking.

Attila on:
"Risk-taking Can Backfire"

In planning my murder, Chrysaphius took enormous
risks. But he also put Vigilas in a position to be blamed
should his conspiracy fail.

Edecon reported the plot for my murder to Orestes and
myself. We amused ourselves by turning the scheme back on
the Romans. Still, to let Vigilas take all the blame for failing
to see my murder through to its end was wrong of Theodosius, and I told him as much. He was a poor excuse for a
leader—even a Roman one—and he let his grand eunuch
escape punishment.

When Theodosius died, he was succeeded by Marcian, a
professional soldier and a leader of some mettle who held
his subordinates accountable for their own actions. Marcian
knew how Vigilas had paid for the grand eunuch's ill-considered plan to have me assassinated by my own trusted chieftains and warriors. He also knew that Chrysaphius was
skilled at shifting blame for his mistakes to others. I must say

that I admire Marcian for holding people accountable. For example, one of his first official acts as emperor was to have Chrysaphius executed.

Risk-taking is intrinsic to leadership. If tribal leaders don't take risks, our nation will not progress. Risk-taking involves making a decision and charting a course of action where there is uncertainty about eventual success. And chieftains who avoid making even routine decisions risk tenure as tribal leaders.

Among our tribes and in our nation, I believe that the degree of risk one is expected to take should be commensurate with his or her office. The higher the office, the greater the risks. Further, among Huns, warriors are not expected to take blame for the actions of a chieftain. There are no cover-ups, no lies, no deceptions. Whoever is responsible for achieving less than expected faces the consequences of failure. Conversely, whoever is responsible for excelling reaps the rewards of success. Listen now to my thoughts on taking risks.

- Chieftains who expect warriors or Huns to take arrows for them breed corruption. No chieftain has the right to blame subordinates for his or her mistakes.

- Every good and excellent thing Huns can accomplish carries within it the potential for failure.

- A tribe without a chieftain and warriors that are willing to take risks never achieves greatness.

- Huns may be surprised to discover that many great chieftains are haunted, from time to time, by the fear of failure.

- When chieftains punish their warriors and Huns for honest mistakes, they accomplish at least two bad things: First, they kill initiative; second, they discourage future risk-taking.

- Playing it safe and avoiding risks are major reasons that the Roman Empire is crumbling before us. Leaders over Huns must not be averse to taking appropriate risks.

- The essence of risk-taking is acting without assurance that you have all the relevant facts.

- Early success as a risk-taker is dangerous if it leads a chieftain to be overconfident in taking greater risks in the future.

- Chieftains reap the rewards of their tribes' successes. They should also be accountable for their tribes' problems and failures.

- Chieftains who allow subordinates to cover up mistakes for them compromise their followers' ability to fulfill their responsibilities effectively and objectively.

- Huns who avoid difficult assignments would make poor warriors and worse chieftains.

- A chieftain who focuses more sharply on blame for the creation of a problem than on its solution teaches warriors and Huns to avoid responsibility.

And with this last thought, we shall end our meeting:

- Huns who never fail are ill prepared to deal with the bitterness and disappointment they will encounter as warriors. All warriors fail from time to time, but failing never stops a warrior from pursuing victory.

Chieftains, do not avoid risks in the execution of your duties. I know that because you take risks, you will occasionally fail. Learn from each failure. Teach others how to avoid mistakes. Accept accountability for your actions, and hold your subordinate leaders accountable for theirs. Risk-taking is a skill that is never totally mastered. Go now, and teach these principles to your warriors and Huns.

XII

Trust

"Honor-as-armor"

Although his realm was constantly threatened by barbarian invasions, Theodosius II was neither a politician nor a warrior. Quite the contrary, a man of friendly and gentle disposition, he is said to have frequently signed official papers without so much as skimming them. His only significant display of statesmanship and military zeal came when he declared his cousin Valentinian III emperor in the West upon the death of Honorius, then sent his military forces to reclaim the imperial purple in Ravenna for the Theodosian dynasty.

Most of the time, Theodosius was somewhat cowardly when it came to war. Rather than commanding his generals to answer invasions with arms, Theodosius secured peace by paying tribute to the barbarian invaders (principally the Huns). Perhaps his lack of aggression had its source in the death of his father, Arcadius, when Theodosius was only seven. He succeeded his father on the throne in the East, but because of his youth, he was left in the care of Antiochus, a palace eunuch. Until the emperor came of age, Theodosius' court was administered by the praetorian prefect, Anthemius. His ministers and generals were competent but corrupt men whose sordid dissension and cunning treachery were motivated by avarice and lust for power. When Theodosius finally took over the reins of government, these men outwitted and manipulated him to their own ends.

The forty-two years of Theodosius' reign (the longest in the history of the Roman Empire) were marred by chaos, corruption, and court intrigues—conditions under which trust among leaders becomes an increasingly rare and valuable asset.

As told earlier, when Chrysaphius told Theodosius that they would soon be rid of Attila, the world's greatest menace, the emperor was incredulous because he was accustomed to betrayal in his own court but believed the Huns were loyal to Attila. And they were!

Trust was what enabled Attila to unite the independent Hunnic tribes into a strong confederacy. Tribal chieftains had to trust Attila to make good his promises. In return, Attila had to trust these chieftains to be loyal to him and to his plan for a Great Conquest. Moreover, as the Huns assimilated many foreigners into their nation, Attila and his subordinate leaders had to learn how far to trust these strangers, some of whom were Roman spies.

In forging his new nation, Attila took risks. Since those he appointed as leaders would often speak for the Hunnic nation, his chieftains must be shrewd and trustworthy. If they were not, they would quickly undo all his diligent work.

Attila recognized the importance of trust in building both solid personal relationships and winning organizations. The king of Huns wished his warriors to be successful as chieftains, so he taught them the meaning of trust.

Attila on:
"Honor-as-armor"

Tonight you warriors are here to gain from my insights into the significance of trust for our tribes and nation. The Roman Empire was once great and powerful. But now in

Ravenna as well as in Constantinople, its impotent emperors are burdened with ministers and advisors that are not trustworthy. Chrysaphius, the grand eunuch of Theodosius, typified the men of whom I speak.

A coward among cowards, Chrysaphius was quick to advise Theodosius to pay me large sums of gold, grant me territories, and return Hunnic runaways in return for peace with our nation. I willingly accepted these terms of peace because winning by diplomatic means is always the option of first choice. I might also add here that the Romans call these payments of tribute extortion. But I say no. When the Romans decided to expand the boundaries of their nation, they took lands through the might of their armies. Then, after conquering new frontiers, the Romans demanded annual tribute from their new subjects. In return, the Romans promised these people peace. The land and money they took they called taxes. But when we took their gold, they called it extortion. The Romans have always had a strange way of justifying their own behavior. I call it a double standard.

Now, getting back to Chrysaphius—Constantinople's treasury began to run dry, so the grand eunuch wanted to stop paying the tribute to me that preserved the peace. In Edecon, he thought he had found a Hun who was as corrupt as he, who would do anything for gold, even kill me. He was wrong to judge Edecon, a Hun, by the low standards of conduct the Romans hold for themselves.

Edecon would have been neither a chieftain nor an ambassador if he were corruptible. Just as I can ill afford to have friends whom I cannot completely trust, our nation cannot prosper without leaders in whom we can place total trust.

To be trusted is to be honored. Trust is the basis of strong relationships between friends and colleagues alike. As future chieftains, you must learn to trust and to be trustworthy. Listen now as I give you my counsel on honor—on doing the right thing.

• Chieftains who expect their warriors and Huns to trust them should first trust their warriors and Huns.

• Corrupt chieftains not only tarnish their own reputations but also cast suspicion on the reputations of honest chieftains.

• Although a well-trained Hun won't always make the best choice, an untrained Hun is not likely to know a good choice from a bad one. Chieftains who don't train Huns to make wise choices suffer the consequences.

• It is a prudent chieftain who promises only that which can be delivered and who then commits the tribe's resources to delivering all that has been promised.

• Chieftains who meet their Huns' needs—even at their own expense—are honorable leaders.

• As a chieftain's responsibilities increase, he or she must rely more on subordinate leaders to watch over the Huns. But no worthy chieftain ever relies on an untrustworthy subordinate.

• High-handed chieftains thrive on confrontation with easily defeated foes. They also demand total control, have closed minds, and make terrible leaders. We need high-minded chieftains, not high-handed ones.

• Secrets are exposed as soon as they are known to three Huns or to one Roman.

• When chieftains suggest that a warrior or Hun compromise his or her beliefs, they are really asking the warrior or Hun to surrender integrity. Once such compromises begin, they become easier to suggest and harder to refuse.

• Chieftains do well to remember that if they expect perfection from themselves, they may become overly critical of warriors and Huns who fail to achieve perfection. But warriors and Huns who do the best they can yet fail to achieve perfect results should be treated with respect.

• Chieftains, warriors, and Huns who are vulgar and unpleasant gain neither trust nor respect.

• Without rules to regulate their behavior, highly competitive chieftains and warriors become abusive, commit ruthless acts, and fight over minor issues.

• Huns must be trained to serve the tribe's interests, so that when they are tempted to make a quick personal gain at the expense of the tribe, they will instead do as they have been taught.

• Chieftains don't always know when they are doing the wrong thing. Even when they do know, they may be so caught up in the passions of the moment that they fail to consider the consequences of their wrongdoing. Therefore, chieftains need advisors they trust to remind them of the potential consequences of ill-considered actions.

• In order to fulfill the expectations of office, a chieftain is sometimes a very different person in public from the person he or she is in private. But no worthy chieftain disgraces the title even in private.

• Chieftains who encourage their Huns to cheat in order to win rob them of the joy of winning fairly.

• Huns prone to political maneuvering may gain power and influence by appearing to have abilities that they in fact lack. Before these Huns are revealed for what they are, they can cause a lot of damage to their tribes. So be on the lookout for them.

I now conclude my counsel on honor-as-armor with one last thought:

• The deepest scars a Hun bears are not of the body, but of the soul. Wounds to the body heal faster and more thoroughly than those inflicted on the soul—and they are less threatening to the good of the Hun, his or her tribe, and the nation.

Now you warriors have the benefit of my wisdom on the honor-as-armor that goes hand in hand with trust. There will be a few Huns and many Romans in your future who will be of questionable character. For selfish gains, they will betray all they profess to honor. You must quickly establish who these are and treat them with suspicion unless their behavior changes consistently for the better. Concerning all others, learn to trust them, and you, too, will be trusted. When you return to your tribes tomorrow, remember these lessons well.

XIII

Easy Wins

"Lucky Breaks Aren't Just Good Luck"

In 450, after years of detailed planning and preparation, Attila summoned Ardaric, king of the Gepids, and Theodemir, king of the Ostrogoths—his principal allies—to his palace at Etzelnburg. It was time for the Huns to begin the Great Conquest. This campaign was against the Western Empire alone. But Marcian had succeeded Theodosius II to the throne of the Eastern Roman Empire that same year. And he had abruptly ceased paying tribute to the Huns. Although his army really was not prepared to face the swelling horde that now stretched from the Danube to the Hercynian forest, Marcian was determined to defeat Attila and spare his treasury and his subjects the high price of peace.

Attila—who saw the conquest of Ravenna as a stepping-stone in the Great Conquest—proceeded West, where he believed inhabitants would be less belligerent and determined to resist him than in the East. Attila always preferred to win without striking a blow. Why risk losing any valuable soldiers in battle with the Eastern Romans over the unpaid tribute?

In January of 451, Attila's vast army began an assault on the Western Roman Empire. As Attila advanced, he sent out word that there would be no pillaging. Citizens of local tribes, hamlets, and villages had nothing to fear from his massive array of Mongols, Germans, and Slavs. All peoples who allied with the Huns not only would be freed of Roman

subjugation but also would have their ancient independence restored. Conversely, any who resisted the Huns or
assisted the Western Romans would be annihilated.

The advance of the Huns was accompanied by a clamorous din of battle cries, victory songs, pounding hooves,
clanking swords, cracking whips, and rumbling chariots. Attila and his battlefield commanders had organized their
horde into disciplined and well-led units. Like a human
tidal wave, they surged over fields, forests, and streams. The
scene was panoramic—a mighty army of heterogeneous yet
single-minded warriors in native war-fighting dress, speaking native languages.

The Burgundians, Thuringians, and Franks offered no
resistance, and many of them joined Attila's ranks. The
Huns had anticipated an ambush at the Rhine. None occurred. A few minor battles were fought along the way, and
then Attila passed under Porta Nigra and was well on his
way to Rome. He soundly defeated Gunther, who commanded an army of Burgundians and Salian Franks. As a
result of Gunther's decision to fight, the Huns destroyed
Worms, Windisch, Spires, and Mayence. Attila's army rode
forward in what many scholars of war consider to be the
most rapid cavalry advance in the history of warfare. Luck?
Maybe. The result of well-thought-out and carefully executed plans? More likely.

Encouraging the Huns to rely on preparation rather than
on good luck, Attila spoke to his chieftains and warriors
about their responsibilities in getting themselves and their
Huns ready to win on the battlefield.

Attila on:
"Lucky Breaks Aren't Just Good Luck"

The swift westward advance of our Great Conquest in 451
was not the result of good fortune. Our armies and those of
our allies were prepared to win. We promised that where no

resistance was made, no harm would come. We kept our word and neither looted nor disturbed the land.

I was well aware of how the Roman army had deteriorated in the West. But I did not want to confront the renowned Aëtius. So I informed the Romans that our plan was to march into Gaul against the Visigoths. I deceived them of our real intention, which was to take Ravenna. After that, we would collect the tribute due us from Constantinople.

Our advance was remarkably smooth considering the problems inherent in moving so large an army. We were prepared to win, but we did not let the enemy know what we were up to. I was pleased with how quickly we moved and with the discipline of our army, for we did not loot or burn the cities we passed along the way. But finally, at Orléans, our discipline broke. Soon afterward we fought Aëtius and his Visigoth and Alani allies on the Catalaunian Plains and lost to them, for we withdrew first. But our success had held until we lost discipline at Orléans.

Aëtius' ability to thwart our advance in Gaul had nothing to do with our running out of luck, for it wasn't chance that gave our horde swift and successful victories. Our calamity was a transient lapse in responsible leadership. Now heed my words, which will remind you that we need not accept such a fate again.

• Many opportunities to change the course of battle come from unexpected sources. Chieftains who have learned how to recognize opportunity, and warriors and Huns who have been trained to respond to unexpected circumstance, prosper from a stroke of good luck.

• Huns prepared to win are awesome competitors regardless of the outcome of the battle.

• No chieftain, warrior, or Hun has many job assignments that are fun or frivolous. Most of what they do that provides long-term benefits for them or the tribe is tedious, difficult, and time-consuming.

• As every superior skill a Hun develops can be turned into an asset, sensible chieftains insist that their Huns be trained by the best warriors.

• Weak chieftains prefer unimaginative, inexpensive, and safe action plans. Beyond these, they rely on good luck to bring them success.

• Chieftains can't build strong tribes on weak foundations. Leaving the fate of the tribe to luck places the tribe on a weak foundation. Chieftains, therefore, develop plans and organize activities that strengthen their tribes. But doing so is never easy or cheap.

• Only after they acquire the fundamentals of complicated skills can Huns benefit from watching and working with talented warriors.

• With a poor leader, Huns can only win against foes whose leader is worse.

• Nothing leads to the fall of Huns in battle faster than the absence of their chieftain.

• Winning tribes are led by chieftains who understand that no tribe is lucky enough to meet only less well-led opponents.

• When riding into battle with untrained warriors and Huns, a chieftain can be certain that very few of them will perform well.

• After an incompetent chieftain is exposed, the Huns will never believe him or her to be genuine without profound improvement in the quality of leadership.

• When chieftains are fortunate enough to have lots of time to make a decision, they should never hurry to commit to a particular course of action.

• Warriors and Huns whose chieftains are skeptical are lucky, because these leaders tend to make good decisions.

- Neither chieftain nor warrior can control future opportunities to win, but they can seize the opportunities they encounter each day.

- Chieftains and warriors must be curious, observant, analytical, and sensitive to change in order to prevail over formidable foes.

Finally:

- For chieftain and warrior alike, not all distinction or booty is earned. So when you benefit from good fortune, don't try to convince others that your advantage was earned by skill.

Now you chieftains and warriors have my counsel on what it takes to win. Believing that you can win without preparation and sacrifice is a costly mistake. When you rely on chance alone, you will lose many battles. Winning is what being a Hun is all about. And it is your charge as tribal leaders to return to your camps and prepare your Huns to win.

XIV

Headaches

"You Get Paid for Your Bad Days"

In the spring of 451, Attila led a colossal horde consisting of Mongolian, Slavic, and Germanic warriors in a relentless march on the Western Empire. His army rode forward at breakneck speed, passing peacefully through villages that offered no resistance, demolishing those that did. Warned of the immense barbarian army riding toward them, the Roman army abandoned its frontier garrisons and retreated to the west. The Empire's barbarian mercenaries, who remained along the frontier, offered little resistance to the onslaught of the Hunnic horde. Fear of Attila's troops won battles before they began. The forces of the king of Huns galloped forward with precision and discipline, sustained by easy victories. Their courage persisted. Their confidence was great. Attila appreciated this opportunity for his troops to develop the habit of success, for he expected them to need a deep reservoir of strength when they encountered Aëtius' forces in the early summer.

In April, Attila's army reached Metz. Surrounded by high walls, it was a superbly fortified and well-provisioned city governed by a bishop, who was himself a warrior of some mettle. The bishop refused to open the gates of his city to the Huns. Attila responded as he always did to resistance during this campaign—he launched an attack. His warriors were virtually impossible to defeat in open warfare. What they lacked in weapons and training, the barbarian warriors made up for in fighting spirit. The professional army of the

Western Empire, however, had catapults, siege machines, unity of action, and command organization. In a siege, the Huns were inferior warriors.

The horde showered the walls of Metz with arrows, from which the garrisoned soldiers easily protected themselves with metal shields. The defenders, in turn, poured flaming pitch and boiling oil and water down on the Hunnic forces, who were ill prepared to scale walls. The Huns battered the city's gates with logs, but to no avail. The harder the Hunnic troops fought, the more resolved the soldiers of Metz became. As the siege grew longer, more and more Huns were killed or seriously injured. Exasperated, Attila decided to bypass Metz. It wasn't tactically sound to leave an armed enemy at your rear, but the siege was breaking the rhythm of the horde's march and was undermining its habit of success. He wanted to turn his back on this unpleasant and difficult situation.

Lifting his siege, Attila pressed forward only to learn a few days later that part of the wall around Metz had finally fallen as a result of the Huns' assault. Soldiers were vigorously working to repair the break. In a move that took the soldiers of Metz by surprise, Attila turned his army around and on Easter night attacked the city once more. By Monday's dawn, the only building that stood in Metz was a single church.

Attila was usually tenacious. He often prevailed in spite of onerous obstacles. But he recognized that his young leaders did not yet understand, as he did, that leading the Huns through their bad days—working hard under duress—is what a chieftain is compensated to do. To that end he spoke with his young tribal leaders.

Attila on:
"You Get Paid for Your Bad Days"

Sometimes when everything is going well, you think nothing can go wrong. Then along comes a setback that shatters your day. This was the case at the beginning of our Great Conquest when I led the Huns across the Rhine on our stampede into Gaul. Metz became an obstacle that halted our rapid advance and undercut the morale of the horde.

We besieged Metz, pounding its massive walls without effect. Rather than persist, I convinced myself to move on without devoting the time and resources to taking Metz that were called for. That was the wrong thing to do. You should never leave an armed enemy at your back. And you should never give up when you can still persist.

As king of Huns, my duty was, and is, to see the horde through its bad days—in that case, to take Metz and not give up because the job was tough. You young chieftains and warriors must understand that if everything is going smoothly, a leader need not step forward and interrupt the course of events. But when events turn on the Huns, strong and able leadership must reverse the course. Leaders are paid to lead on bad days, not to abdicate when challenged—and not to take credit for easy victories.

In returning to defeat Metz, I had the good fortune to redeem my lapse of responsibility toward the Huns. You cannot rely on such luck, so I offer you these words of counsel on working through your bad days.

• The best way to accomplish an assignment is efficiently and effectively. Unfortunately, the efficacious path is rarely clear at the start of difficult, complicated assignments.

• A good chieftain recognizes that moments of stark terror can be reduced by finding a practical approach to whatever produces them.

- A Hun's duties include unglamorous, difficult, and sometimes monotonous tasks. A chieftain's duty is to see that these tasks are accomplished in a timely fashion.

- Some jobs in battle are more enjoyable than others, but all jobs must be done before we enjoy the fruits of victory.

- The best Huns perform at their peak against the best competition. Victories over weak competitors do not prepare Huns to win against tough competition.

- The only thing Huns will develop by not trying to win against challenging competition is a habit of losing.

- Putting off today's decisions can ruin tomorrow.

- Huns become hostages to unconquered fears. The finest Huns, therefore, overcome their fears and courageously confront frightening situations.

- Chieftains who pay heed to small, annoying problems find that fewer large, threatening problems arise.

- Making excuses for not making decisions is a sign to the Huns that the chieftain is no longer in charge.

- If Huns could overcome all of their problems by themselves, being the chieftain would not be the full-time occupation it is.

- Chieftains who do not learn from their bad days—when they fail on the battlefield—founder more often than chieftains who do profit from negative experiences. Repeated defeat opens old wounds and leads to despair and disillusionment.

- Wise chieftains toil in the present to teach the Huns to solve their own problems in the future.

- When a chieftain tells a Hun whose performance is substandard what he or she must do to meet expectations, it is a great day. When a chieftain fails to tell a poorly performing Hun how to meet expectations, it is a bad day. In the first instance, the Hun learns that the chieftain is not happy and what steps to take to make the chieftain happy. In the second instance, the Hun learns only that the chieftain is not happy.

• When I hear a chieftain, warrior, or Hun question whether or not learning something new and useful is worth the effort, I like to remind him or her that the uneducated are at the mercy of those who know the answers.

• Even the dullest of Huns realizes that making the effort to learn how to ride a horse into battle is better than confronting the enemy on foot.

• Chieftains who complain of too many bad days are reminded that "tough" is when you have no place left to turn.

• Chieftains who habitually rant and rave are ineffective leaders. Huns who periodically bitch and complain are just being Huns—it is their way of handling frustration.

• All arrogant chieftains will learn this humbling lesson—a serious defeat has a very direct way of helping you take notice of your limits.

And I close our assembly tonight with this thought:

• Chieftains who surrender too early don't understand that victory is often won late in battle. Winning chieftains don't give up easily.

Now that I have spoken, enjoy the food and drink that has been prepared for you. After you have partaken, rest, and on the morrow, return to your tribes. Remember that earning your booty as a tribal leader is more demanding than it was as a follower. More is expected of you now. Naturally, after some battles you'll get great booty with very little effort—for whatever reason—and after other long, arduous fights, you'll feel your booty is far less than it should be. The fact is, over time, you'll get paid about as much booty as you earn. So don't waste your time complaining.

XV

Getting Close Enough

"Approximating the Answer"

Soon after the Huns laid waste to Metz, they seized and routed Rheims, Laon, and St. Quentin. Attila's campaign was progressing as planned, and the road to Lutetia (Paris) was now clear for his intrepid Hunnic cavalry.

Although the Lutetians had been oppressed by the Romans (who had abolished their freedoms, banished their gods, and dethroned their kings), they feared the Hunnic barbarians more than any other enemy. They knew their own meager forces were no match for Attila's massive army. At first they hoped to avoid a fate worse than Roman subjugation by aligning themselves with Aëtius' imperial forces. The confidence of the men of Lutetia that Aëtius would protect them, however, was soon shaken to the core.

Tales arrived at Lutetia daily of the mayhem the Huns unleashed on towns and villages opposing them. Exaggerated or not, this news fed the panic that flickered when the arrival of Aëtius' army was delayed; the panic flared when Hunnic scouts were seen reconnoitering on the bank of the Seine across from Lutetia. Terrified that their city would not be protected from Attila's rapidly advancing forces, the men of Lutetia began to prepare for an evacuation of the city.

In contrast, the women of Lutetia believed they would be spared destruction at the hands of the barbarians, so they refused to flee. The steadfast courage of these women was based on religious faith. According to legend, Geneviève (a woman honored for her piety) prophesied that Lutetia would not fall to Attila, so there was nothing to fear. While the gutless men bundled together their possessions in preparation for evacuating the city, the women (although threatened by the men with beatings) met in the Baptistery of St. Jean-le-Rond to join Geneviève in prayer and hymn singing.

Too cowardly to fight in defense of their city, the men of Lutetia were brave enough to storm the baptistery's massive locked doors in an attempt to forcibly remove their women. The resulting pandemonium moved a priest to ask the men their intentions. When they said they wanted to gather their women and retreat from the city, the priest protested that Geneviève was a saint and her advice was, therefore, trustworthy. The moderating influence of the priest's reassurances quieted their fears. Told that their men were now determined to stand by them, the women opened the gates of the church, and everyone returned to their homes.

Meantime, Attila had received word that Theodoric, king of the Visigoths, intended to join forces with Aëtius in an effort to stop the advance of the Huns. A master of battlefield tactics, the king of Huns knew he must reach the forces of Theodoric before Aëtius arrived. Determined to avoid the overwhelming threat that a combined Roman-Visigoth army would pose to him, Attila decided to bypass Lutetia, because under the circumstances, capturing this city no longer had a high priority. As he turned his vast horde southward, Attila intended to ride at breakneck speed straight to Toulouse (the Visigoth capital). It was in order to get to Toulouse before Aëtius did that Attila spared Lutetia. But his reason mattered little to the Lutetians, who, as soon as the Huns disappeared from their countryside, chanted a Te Deum in the baptistery in Geneviève's honor.

The Lutetians felt justified in having acted on the women's faith in Geneviève's prophecy. Attila felt justified in bypassing Lutetia and moving with urgency toward a more important tactical objective—meeting Theodoric at Toulouse to propose a Hun-Visigoth alliance before Theodoric could join his forces with those of Aëtius.

But the Huns were sidetracked from their goal by a fateful desire to capture and sack Orléans—a time-consuming enterprise. Had the Huns stuck to their original plan, they might never have been pitted against the combined army of the Romans and the Visigoths as they were—first at Orléans (which they had defeated and were still savaging) and later on the Catalaunian Fields, where they fought to a draw but were the first to retreat from the bloody battle.

Attila became a wise and seasoned leader by learning from this and other experiences that a chieftain must not give in to the temptation to gain a small win that may reduce his chance to gain a large competitive advantage over the enemy. The heart of the matter had been to prevent the unification of the Roman and Visigoth armies, as Attila knew all too well. Sacking another city—no matter what its treasures—was self-indulgent and costly.

In his waning years, the king of Huns wanted future Hunnic leaders to profit from his own hard-won wisdom, so once again he gathered some of his promising warriors in counsel.

Attila on:
"Approximating the Answer"

As future chieftains, you young warriors will be confronted by complicated decisions that you may base on either erroneous data or a predisposition to stick with past practices. Even I, your king, have been troubled by this inherent weakness in a leader's decision-making process. Moreover, I have approximated correct answers only to be sidetracked later from following through on my decisions. Even when I knew how to achieve a competitive advantage over our political and battlefield enemies, I did not always persevere. You will find as leaders that you cannot assume that all the relevant facts are available to you when you are making decisions—if they were, you could quite possibly

make perfect decisions! Because every variable bearing on
the problem is not known in advance, the rare perfect decision isn't recognizable until long after it is made. All of you
are potential chieftains of our tribes, and some of you will
rise to positions of great leadership in our nation. You,
therefore, deserve the full benefit of my own experience in
arriving at solutions that—while not necessarily perfect—
are close enough.

As I reflect on the advance of our mighty army on Lutetia, I now understand that it was never an important city to
conquer. The Lutetians posed no serious obstacle to our
advance. Fortunately, I avoided wasting our resources on
the sack of Lutetia, although I suspect we would have enjoyed carting off its treasures.

I assumed that Theodoric might prefer joining forces
with us to collaboration with the Romans. He knew that the
Romans let barbarians do most of the fighting for them;
therefore, the burden of battle with our vast army would fall
on his Visigoth warriors. I was determined to convince
Theodoric that siding with us against Aëtius' army was his
only hope of escaping a mighty defeat in battle with us. As it
turned out, the subsequent damage Aëtius brought on our
forces was made possible by Theodoric's reinforcement of
the Roman army, first at Orléans and later on the Catalaunian Fields. Obviously, my original decision to reach
Theodoric before his alliance with Aëtius could be consum-
mated was correct. Where I erred was in abandoning this
decision and instead indulging in our accustomed practice
of laying waste to towns along the way.

Orléans was a fortified city ruled by a determined and
pugnacious bishop. He put up a great fight before we finally
took his city. After our long and arduous siege, I foolishly
allowed my army to pillage and plunder the city. While this
had been an acceptable habit in the past, at Orléans it
robbed us of an alliance with the Visigoths and of a victory
against the Roman Empire. Moreover, there had been only
feeble defensive forces garrisoned within the well-fortified

walls at Orléans. No mobile cavalry would have threatened our advance straight past Orléans to Toulouse, where Theodoric waited.

But that is all in the past. What was done is done. You must learn to cut to the heart of any matter and abandon traditions that no longer support your competitive advantage. Listen now as I tell you the essence of approximating answers and avoiding pitfalls as you define, prioritize, and achieve your objectives.

• When making time-sensitive decisions, chieftains adopt long-term strategies and short-term tactics that help them attain the desired outcome regardless of what worked in the past.

• Huns rarely concern themselves with the motives and goals of the enemy. Warriors prepare themselves to win against motivated and goal-oriented enemies. Chieftains understand the motives and goals of the opposition; armed with this insight, they frame strategies and determine tactics that will undermine the competition's strengths and exploit its weaknesses.

• Huns want their leaders to make perfect decisions. Warriors fret over the possibility of making poor decisions. Chieftains intellectually and emotionally process all the available information that they consider relevant in order to decide wisely for the tribe.

• At the time they are made, tough decisions are neither black nor white, and there are many gradations of gray. Nonetheless, chieftains who base tough decisions on what needs to be accomplished in order to achieve long-term tribal goals rarely lead their followers down a path of ruin.

• Huns aren't paid to make decisions for the tribe. Warriors would like to be paid to make decisions for the tribe. Chieftains are paid to make proactive, not reactive, decisions that produce positive results for the Huns.

- When chieftains recognize a threat to their tribes, they respond immediately—before their attention is diverted to lesser issues and their ability to act effectively is undermined.

- Once committed to a course of action that will benefit their tribes, chieftains must press forward and see it through. Chieftains who neglect this responsibility find that meaningless activity replaces their tribes' purposeful pursuits.

- Most Huns will follow competent chieftains into even the most dangerous situations. Able warriors will volunteer for the most difficult and challenging missions. Seasoned chieftains will lead their tribes only where they need to go.

- Huns usually approach a task as they have been trained to do. Warriors often believe there is only one way to accomplish a task—their way! Chieftains who visualize several ways to accomplish a task before choosing one increase the odds that it will be accomplished successfully.

- More often than not, even the best battle plans become obsolete once the fighting begins.

- Anticipation of the unexpected gives leaders a competitive edge.

- It is not the amount of time but rather the quality of thought devoted to solving a problem that determines how soon and how well it will be solved.

- Huns rarely understand the subtleties of complex problems. Warriors too often allow subtleties to obscure the solution. Chieftains who understand the subtleties of a problem expedite solution.

- Chieftains should never intentionally place Huns in a situation where the price of losing outweighs the rewards of winning.

And by way of concluding my thoughts this night:

- Chieftains who believe they can't influence events have, in fact, surrendered before the battle begins.

Now it is up to you young warriors to heed my words of counsel on approximating the answers to questions you will face as you make decisions in the future. Your ability to do this well will allow you to find solutions, avoid unnecessary distractions, and act wisely despite faulty, inadequate, or erroneous information.

XVI

Quality

"A Few Good Warriors"

Two Hun warriors had been sent to meet a distinguished Roman army officer recently estranged from the Empire and to lead him back to Attila's camp. Their hair was cut in a circular manner, after the Hunnic fashion, and was tucked under small leather caps. Clad in heavy garments of fur, the two beardless escorts rode ahead of the Roman on thin, shaggy ponies. The Huns were armed with technically perfect war bows that were permanently strung, were reflexed, and were distinguished by seven bone plaques that stiffened the ears and handle. Lightly equipped, neither one wore body armor or a metal helmet, nor did either carry a shield. No matter, for their mission was peaceful.

The trio's serpentine route took them past bustling hamlets and over quiet rivers, which they crossed on rafts that local habitants had tied to bushes near the water's edge. Finally, they reached an opening in a thick stand of forest from which the Roman officer (whose name is not now known) had his first glimpse of the city where the palace of the king of Huns stood. He was surprised by how primitive this center of power was, and he approached it with curiosity.

As the trio entered the huge gates of the wooden stockade that surrounded the city, the Roman surveyed the scene before him. Two-wheeled wains wended their way among tents and wooden houses. Children were everywhere—playing, running, and fighting. Young women tended cauldrons that bubbled over open fires and scented the air with pungent aromas. In numerous small workshops, artisans crafted wooden saddles, long lances, javelins, plaited cloth lassos, bone-and-horn body armor reinforced with metal, metal helmets, bows, bone- or metal-tipped arrows, lightly armored wickerwork shields, daggers, and swords. Dogs prowled in packs and barked warnings to each other. Horses and livestock were so loosely confined that pedestrians had to watch their steps.

As the travelers came to a halt near the middle of the camp, one of the warriors called the officer's attention to two men walking toward them. They were to take him to the royal palace, where Attila awaited him.

Attila's palace was the largest and finest wooden structure in the Hunnic city. Adjacent to the palace stood quarters for his many wives and bodyguards. The Roman officer was escorted into a large hall where Attila sat on a wooden stool. The king of Huns wore a sword at his side; a bow and a hatchet were within his reach. Attila did not rise to greet his guest. Instead, the Roman was offered a gold-and-silver goblet of wine and was told to drink from it as a salute to the Hunnic king. In response Attila drank from a wooden cup, saluting the Roman.

During the interview, Attila questioned the Roman officer in detail. Where and under whom had the officer served? How many men had he led? What training procedures did he employ? What were his methods of discipline? Why was he deserting the Roman army at this point in his career? Didn't he value the pension that the Roman Empire must pay him for his twenty years of service? What about the free land and the tax relief he was entitled to as a Roman army veteran?

Did he believe that the Huns could learn to use catapults fashioned after those employed by the Roman legions? Could the Huns learn to forgo plunder and pillage as the principal rewards of battle and fight instead for expansion of the cause of the Hunnic nation? Could he teach the

newly formed Hunnic infantry to march in serried pha-
lanxes as did the Roman infantry? (Attila wanted his Hunnic foot soldiers to march with the discipline shown by the
Roman army of old—three feet between each pair of
soldiers, six feet between ranks.) And could the officer
teach the Huns to use the shield and slings as effectively as
they employed their bows? Could he even teach the Huns to
use the siege machines that would enable them to conquer
city fortresses—until now impregnable to the Hunnic cavalry?

Attila was a keen judge of men, and he was not one to
restrict the honor and privilege of leadership to men of his
own blood. But placing outsiders over his Huns would have
discouraged them had they not realized that their king
never acted capriciously when selecting his leaders.
Onegesius, second in command over the Huns, was Greek.
Orestes, another member of Attila's inner circle, was a Pannonian. Attila even welcomed Gallic chieftains into the
horde. They were joined by African, Celtic, German, Greek,
Persian, and Spanish warriors. Attila was keen on including
any and all who offered loyal, competent service in the
cause of the Huns. He appreciated talent wherever he
found it, and he had a rare ability to use it to further the
best interests of his nation.

One of Attila's major ambitions was to build the most
powerful army the world had ever known. Strong, resource-
ful, well-trained, and highly motivated warriors were essential to his plan for completing the Great Conquest. These
warriors would endure hardship without complaint. They
would perform even routine duties with rare intensity. Less
talented men might be threatened and intimidated by them
but nonetheless would emulate them. Attila understood
how to harness the independent spirits of these warriors
without limiting their potential. And from among the best
of them, he would choose leaders who dared to stand and
fight against any odds.

To forge the raw talents and abilities of his best warriors

into highly skilled, disciplined leadership, the services of a
master teacher were required. The Roman officer who now
sat before Attila could do the job. He intended to cast his lot
with the Huns because he was tired of the Roman citizens'
ingratitude and of the emperor's indifference to his faithful
service. He was tired, too, of the corruption and intrigue
played out daily in the court at Ravenna. He could and
would help Attila hone his army into a winning war machine. Attila was not inclined to turn down such an offer.
This Roman officer was the master teacher to shape the new
Hunnic army.

Attila believed that although training was essential for all
Huns, the selection and development of warriors was one of
the most important duties a chieftain performed. The ongo-
ing and future success of any organization requires the presence of capable and ambitious warriors. For this reason,
Attila counseled his chieftains on their need to staff their
tribes with good warriors.

Attila on:
"A Few Good Warriors"

You chieftains are gathered here to be instructed in staff-
ing your tribes with competent warriors. Long ago, I
learned that no matter how rich a nation is in booty gained
through battle, taxes, or trade, it will soon be impoverished
if no experienced and eager warriors stand ready to step in
as future leaders.

With this in mind, I once welcomed into our nation a
competent and wise Roman army officer. He became one of
those who trained our Huns and warriors in superior battlefield tactics. This is a lesson that you must learn well: One
good warrior makes a difference in a tribe's ability to win,
and more good warriors make more of a difference.

Within our tribes are warriors who get both the best assignments and the most difficult ones. Although these men are usually exciting to be around, at times they are overbearing and obnoxious. On any given day, they may be either punished for their independence or rewarded with extra booty for their exceptional performance. They are imitated by other warriors and admired by Huns. And they are among our nation's ablest leaders!

You should know that such warriors are demanding not only of themselves but also of those Huns around them. They bring a personal intensity to their work that is difficult for others to understand, and they are impatient with fools. They keep informed on developments within their tribe and our nation. They also stay informed about our enemies. Normally, their behavior is within acceptable limits, but it may become unpredictable and cross the lines of propriety. You chieftains must provide the leadership that helps your warriors control their behavior. Warriors make things happen for your tribes. They know how to collect booty—often without doing battle.

Unfortunately, they also disrupt the tribes. But then, if they didn't, they wouldn't be warriors.

You chieftains must realize that from among such warriors your successors will arise. Begin now to visualize them as powerful future leaders, and do what is necessary to see that they learn well. Do not resent them, for you, too, were once young warriors. And remember, there is only so much that chieftains can do each day. If you are to be great, you must leverage your influence and accomplish the assignments I give you by enlisting the talents of your warriors.

Let the thoughts on warriors I now impart guide you.

• Warriors are the driving force within the tribe. Chieftains should, therefore, choose warriors carefully and point them in the right direction.

• Highly effective chieftains staff their tribes with warriors who outperform the warriors they replace.

• Chieftains should not be reluctant to recruit outstanding warriors from other tribes. Nor should they fear bringing into the nation a proficient Roman willing to align with the cause of the Huns.

• A warrior instinctively wants to outperform every other warrior. To minimize natural conflicts, therefore, a chieftain should not assign too many warriors to any one task.

• When warriors become "one of the pack," they surrender many of the attributes that distinguished them as warriors in the first place.

• A majority of warriors perform their duties well but are not potential chieftains. They provide the stability that distinguishes outstanding tribes.

• For a tribe, one of the more challenging aspects of developing strong and able chieftains is tolerating them while they learn to be Huns, and then supporting them while they acquire experience as warriors.

• A Hun whose basic nature is not that of a warrior lives a tormented life in attempting to become one.

• A promising Hun, dressed in the armor and equipped with the weapons of a warrior, soon begins to act and think like a warrior.

• Chieftains tolerate outspoken and independent warriors who produce outstanding results. Chieftains do not tolerate outspoken and independent warriors who produce ordinary results.

• There are fewer good chieftains to lead than there are tribes to be led. And so it comes to pass that some second-rate chieftains end up in charge.

• Success as a Hun doesn't guarantee success as a warrior. Success as a warrior doesn't guarantee success as a chieftain. But mediocrity as a Hun guarantees failure as a warrior.

And mediocrity as a warrior guarantees failure as a chieftain.

• Chieftains who demand the best from their warriors provide them with opportunities to outperform the competition.

• Any attempt to become the perfect warrior is futile, for no warrior can be perfect.

• It is common for great warriors to alienate not only those warriors but also those chieftains who produce mediocre results.

• Huns who associate with inferior warriors may never even develop the qualities that characterize good Huns, much less the qualities of superior warriors.

• Not all great Huns become warriors. Neither do all great warriors become chieftains. But a mighty tribe always allows proficient Huns and capable warriors to flourish according to their abilities.

• A few warriors—who distinguish themselves with personal courage, bravery, and outstanding performance—clearly soar above the rest of the tribe. These are our heroes. Many warriors—who perform competently and responsibly throughout their careers—do not soar, but they do make a solid contribution. These are the backbone of the tribe. To earn distinction in either group is no small feat in the eyes of a chieftain.

With this one last thought, I conclude my counsel on the need for you chieftains to assemble a staff of good warriors:

• Overcompensated, underperforming chieftains find themselves surrounded by underperforming warriors who expect to be overcompensated.

Our victories in past battles have brought our nation great booty. In exchange for this booty, we obtain food,

clothing, and other goods that we do not now produce ourselves. But we cannot base our future prosperity on the be-
lief that there is an endless supply of booty. Such an idea is
foolish at best. While we must continue to win battles, we
must also become more self-sufficient as a nation. And
achieving both these goals requires our tribes to have a few
good warriors—ones that will make the critical difference in
battle and in leading our nation forward. You chieftains are
charged to see that your tribes have such warriors.

XVII

Deception

"Smoke and Mirrors"

Aëtius led the barbarized Western Roman army to many victories. None, however, were more important to the Empire than his de facto defeat of the Huns in the Battle of Châlons. It was this battle that caused Attila and the Huns to withdraw from Gaul and return to Etzelnburg. Despite the battlefield brilliance with which Aëtius secured Ravenna and the rest of Italy briefly from the Huns, he did not receive the accolades he deserved. The bureaucrats and sycophants in Ravenna were no doubt jealous of this prime minister and master of soldiers in the West. The many ambitious Roman officers who served under him were also jealous and hostile. His accomplishments alone were sufficient to alienate lesser men. His bloodline and his ambition made matters worse.

Aëtius' father was a German from Pannonia. His mother was Latin and the daughter of a rich, influential Roman family. While the Roman administrators of the West were happy to have their wealth protected by a half-Roman with a strong but barbarized army, they were nonetheless threatened by Aëtius' strength.

Even friendly Roman army officers—who not only respected Aëtius' military skills but also loathed the intrigues that his enemies stirred up for their master of soldiers—believed the Roman army should be commanded by one of its own. A procession of barbarian generals had been appointed over them. Despite the fact that these barbarians were clearly superior to Latin-blooded officers in courage, personal integrity, and military skills—or perhaps *because* of this fact—the Romans were prejudiced against them.

Fear of and resentment toward Aëtius were so intense and widespread that the emperor, Valentinian, decided to charge him with treason. But many generals announced in no uncertain terms that they would protect their military leader. Unnerved by the threat of a military uprising against him, Valentinian turned to his eunuch Heraclius and his minister Maximus for help.

Realizing that to submit Aëtius to a public trial for treason would spell disaster for the emperor, Heraclius and Maximus convinced Valentinian to change tactics. Earlier, when Aëtius had proposed that his son, Gaudentius, marry the emperor's daughter, Eudocia, the Roman nobles had seen the move as a blatant attempt by Aëtius to legitimize his German heritage so that one of his family could someday succeed to the throne in the West. Accordingly, Valentinian had rebuffed Aëtius' proposal. The emperor had then told all the unmarried officers whom he wanted to bind closer to him that Eudocia's hand was available. Unwittingly, Valentinian had thus created a situation whereby the successful suitor would have instant, powerful enemies.

His eunuch and minister advised the emperor to take advantage of the situation by announcing that Aëtius' son would marry Eudocia after all. The plot was founded on the assumption that the officers who were courting Eudocia would turn viciously on both Aëtius and his son. Valentinian liked the idea and announced the forthcoming marriage of his daughter to Gaudentius. Aëtius was surprised but pleased by the emperor's change of heart and immediately got caught up in the preparations for his son's royal wedding.

As intended, the news that a daughter of the imperial purple was to marry a grandson of a German soldier enraged the citizens of Ravenna. The emperor used the uproar as an excuse to put the wedding off, and off, and off.

But Aëtius continued to prepare for it. He also became pre-
occupied with the intrigues of his enemies. He no longer
had time for his job as master of soldiers, and he left inspection of garrisons along the Empire's frontiers to subordinate officers. These unworthies made their reports back to
Aëtius without leaving the comfort of their quarters at
L'Aquila. They claimed that all Roman strategic defense
forces were prepared and in place. The truth was that, receiving no relief for months on end, many soldiers had deserted and returned to their homes, leaving bridges and
garrisons unprotected. Meanwhile, the Huns had begun
their march to Rome as a continuation of their Great Conquest.

After his battle with Aëtius at Châlons, Attila had returned to Etzelnburg and reformed his military. The Hunnic army approaching the Italian peninsula now was fully
trained in the phalanx movements and the formations of
the Roman army of old. The Huns were well equipped, carrying siege machines and catapults. Assisted by the Roman
army officer who had deserted the Empire and trained the
Huns, Attila had forged his troops into a disciplined fighting machine.

Attila's advance into Italy in 452 was facilitated by the
conspiracy of Valentinian and his advisors against Aëtius.
Intrigues had not only debilitated and humiliated the only
capable military mind left in the West, but also stirred up
the anger of the citizenry. No one was paying attention to
the defense of Italy. The disorganized Roman army was un-
prepared for the onslaught of destructive Huns headed
their way.

As a child hostage in the court of Honorius, Attila had
seen the turmoil that the emperor, his ministers, and his
generals inflicted upon one another through treachery. He
had also seen the havoc wreaked upon the Empire by incompetent officials who made false reports. The king of
Huns had no tolerance for duplicity among leaders, and he

did not long suffer either chieftain or warrior who attempted to trick him or his other leaders. Late in his life, he took the time to share with future chieftains his knowledge of the advantages as well as the pitfalls of deception.

Attila on:
"Smoke and Mirrors"

Tonight I will counsel you young warriors about the proper use of deception. First, you must understand that duplicity is a deadly game. Let us consider, for example, the emperor Valentinian's plot against his best general, Aëtius. Aëtius is no imbecile and should have realized that the emperor would never allow a daughter of the royal purple to marry the son of a half-German. But Aëtius was blinded by ambition. He neglected his duties to the Empire while his officers filed false reports about the frontiers they pretended to have inspected. In the end, Valentinian's vendetta against Aëtius gave us the advantage, because the Romans were ill prepared for our advance on their homeland. While Aëtius was personally humiliated, Valentinian and his associates suffered even more, because we sacked Aquileia and thereby diminished their empire.

I confess that I have employed deception as a weapon, but only against my enemies. When I sat down to negotiate a treaty with the East Romans in the spring of 450, I agreed to abide by the conditions of our treaty of 448: to return their prisoners, to withdraw from the lands south of the Danube, and to free Vigilas, as well. I allowed the ambassadors to believe that their superior diplomatic prowess had convinced me to make these great concessions to Theodosius. But I deceived them.

In reality, I was moving our armies westward to attack Gaul and didn't want to leave our rear exposed to Roman forces from the East. So I handed to them what they thought was a diplomatic victory. In return, our rear was secured, and it remains so. Theodosius is now dead, and his successor, Marcian, refuses to pay the tribute I have grown accustomed to receiving in return for peace in the East Roman Empire. The new emperor rattles his sword and challenges me to come to Constantinople and collect my tribute if I dare. He has said he will replace Roman gold with the iron of his sword. But he has no army strong enough to make good his words. He is just bluffing. We are in no hurry to attend to him, for he poses no real military threat to us. We will take our time collecting his tribute. Meanwhile, listen now to my thoughts on deception.

• Chieftains worthy of the title never sanction duplicity among their troops. The use of deceit with any but an adversary creates an atmosphere of mistrust and produces even greater problems for the Huns.

• One thing a chieftain should always fear more than doing battle is doing battle when only pretending to be prepared.

• Warriors who take their responsibilities seriously usually accomplish whatever is expected of them. Therefore, they don't have to fabricate or exaggerate their achievements.

• Warriors who resort to political maneuvering to gain advantage over their peers lack the talent to achieve recognition through merit.

• The most successful chieftains are realistic and pragmatic. Denial, self-deceit, and wishful thinking are ultimately fatal for chieftains and their followers.

• A good chieftain never tries to gain approval from the Huns by manipulating them irresponsibly.

• Chieftains do not deceive themselves into thinking that speedy action is a substitute for adequate preparation in dealing with foreseeable obstacles to victory.

• Weakness in a chieftain is always recognized by the tribe despite efforts by sycophants to conceal the leader's inadequacies.

- Chieftains given responsibility without authority are sham leaders. It is far better to remove chieftains from office than to strip them of authority and leave them with only an empty show of power.

- A chieftain should never allow warriors or Huns to learn about events that affect their lives through the grapevine—a conduit for lies.

- A chieftain sustains high morale in the horde by seeing that no warrior or Hun has inside knowledge that can be used to intimidate or deceive the uninformed.

- A lazy Hun may attempt to take credit for the accomplishments of another. A jealous warrior may attempt to take credit for the accomplishments of another. A wise chieftain, however, recognizes both and rewards neither.

- While chieftains shouldn't deceive warriors and Huns, they may misrepresent facts to adversaries, who will be confused by this and kept off balance.

I now conclude my counsel with this thought:

- Chieftains who hold on to power through a cunning mixture of deceit, brutality, and largess are desperate despots. Huns do not follow them. Great warriors refuse to serve them. Decent tribes are diminished by their leadership.

As I say farewell for now, I admonish you leaders to stand vigilant against the practice of duplicity within our tribes and nation, and to stamp it out where you find it. Let us all resolve to use deception sparingly—and only against our enemies.

XVIII

Chieftainship

"Leaders' Diseases and Their Cures"

Tonight I have gathered you tribal leaders together in a private assembly to provide you with essential lessons learned from my varied experiences over many years as king of Huns.

For you chieftains, problem solving is a primary responsibility. But specific problems are not what I have called you here to discuss. Let me only advise you to resolve or manage them before they become compounded.

The problems of which I speak tonight are maladies that especially afflict leaders. You should know that being a leader can make you sick. I will describe diseases that have potentially severe ramifications for you and your tribes. At best, they will make you less effective as leaders of Huns. At worst, they will make you totally ineffective.

My desire is that you and your tribes prosper and do not despair. Therefore, I will now tell how you can prevent or cure conditions and diseases that typically infect chieftains.

• Avarice Dysorexia
Chieftains often develop a perverted appetite for booty—or avarice dysorexia. Booty has its place, and being motivated by the prospect of booty is good for a chieftain as well as for his or her tribe. Who wants to follow a leader who doesn't think increasing the possessions of the Huns is important? But fair play applies here as elsewhere. Chieftains who fill only their own caches with booty—at the expense of the

Huns—are greedy, shameless snakes, and the Huns hate them. Leaders who are loathed by their subordinates are useless.

My remedy for avarice dysorexia will surprise those among you who want to acquire great personal wealth. Enlarge the booty of the Huns who do whatever is expected of them well. For those who excel beyond expectation, enlarge their booty even more. If you do what I suggest, you will soon find two things happening. First, the tribe will be more productive than ever before. Second, the Huns will think you are underpaid and will scream at me to pay you more. And, I, Attila, king of Huns, will meet after this assembly with any of you who doesn't want me to increase your booty.

- **Baseless Anxiety**

When everything goes right, you may wonder why nothing goes wrong. Chieftains who do their jobs well have less to worry about, less to do, and more to be proud of than chieftains who don't. When your capable leadership pays off in a big way, you will have a lot of time and energy to put to use in maintaining the tribe's optimal performance. But baseless anxiety—a dramatically high state of tension—may result when you don't know how to enjoy the harvest of your toil or how to rechannel your energy and talents.

Unwarranted worry is common among accomplished chieftains, but it needn't waste their energy. To heal yourself of baseless anxiety, uncover the hidden source of your nameless dread. If you find that you simply don't know what to do with yourself now that things are going so well, you are a typical victim of this disorder. The cure for baseless anxiety is simple. Relax and enjoy the ride for a day or two. Then, find ways to fill the spare time your success has created. This diverts your attention from counterproductive worries. And it allows you to find activities that can make you an even more successful tribal leader, because you will accomplish more for the Huns. Unfortunately, greater success can ignite baseless anxiety once more. But by then you will know how to deal with it. If you fail to diagnose and treat baseless anxiety, you will fail to meet my expectations for you, which will lead to realistic anxiety.

• Compliance Compulsion

One of a chieftain's duties is to give orders, and one of a Hun's duties is to comply with those orders. But at times, your Huns will fail to carry out your directions as well as you expect—or indeed at all. Do not break out in a sweat. There may be good reasons for not following your orders. I can think of five common ones. First, the Huns may not correctly understand them. Second, the Huns may not have the ability to perform as you've directed. Third, successful performance of the task may require additional supervision. Fourth and fifth, your instructions may be contrary to the Huns' self-interests or so stupid that you couldn't even get a Roman to comply.

Chieftains do not necessarily become afflicted with compliance compulsion, but for those who do, it can be a consuming disease. Compliance compulsion is most common in young tribal leaders who are uncertain about how to use their newly acquired power. The plain fact is that the Huns do not always follow orders. Unless you recognize this, you are destined for difficult times. A leader who is surprised and outraged when the Huns ignore what they've been told many times may simply issue more instructions and so make matters worse. The intensity of such a leader's fury agitates the Huns, and eventually leader and Huns alike act irrationally.

You can avoid a great deal of frustration as a tribal leader if you understand that the Huns will not carry out your instructions perfectly. Accept tasks as satisfactorily completed when the job is good enough but not perfect. When a task you have assigned is not completed at all, do not rant and rave. Analyze the situation and take corrective steps to prevent repetition of the failure. You must also know when to leave a task unfinished and let your Huns walk away from it. Many assignments get started that aren't worth finishing. And above all else, realize that the Huns are there to help you as a leader. You are there to get them thinking, feeling, and acting in ways that benefit the tribe. If you can accomplish this, you will have little to worry about when the Huns occasionally do not comply with your orders.

• Corollary Constriction
As you age, many of you chieftains become too committed to your own point of view. This is worse than the mere dislike of new ideas. As your thinking narrows, you become impatient with any Hun who doesn't agree with you. So you cut yourself off from the insights of learned Huns and thereby restrict your tribe's progress. This is not an easy fault to correct.

For those of you with corollary constriction who want to mend your sorry ways, I have the following advice. Understand that not even I, Attila, king of Huns, know everything. This is why I surround myself with smart chieftains and able advisors. I can deal with bad advice, but I can't act wisely without good advice. I listen when a chieftain or advisor comes forward with a suggestion for me to consider. If I rejected all counsel, soon none would be offered. You can't stay abreast of every development on your own, so you need specialized advisors. Listen to them. If they don't know more about their specialties than you do, replace them. Remember that as the world changes, you must either adapt or become obsolete. Obsolescence is not a quality I reward in my chieftains. Lastly, recall how much you respected that chieftain who, when you were unfledged, listened to your ideas. And should you not want the respect of those you lead, see me after this assembly.

• Courage Dystrophy
Some of you chieftains were severely punished when, as younger leaders, you risked and lost. The experience may have infected you with courage dystrophy. Your courage

atrophied, and you are now afraid to take the risks and act with the bravery expected from a leader. Your malady is understandable and sad. No leader of any age should be brutally reprimanded for taking appropriate risks, for making ordinary mistakes, or for making extraordinary mistakes under unusual circumstances. Your ailment is partly the fault of the leader who abused you and partly your own doing, because you continued to serve under a leader afflicted with suffering syndrome and perhaps with compliance compulsion, too.

Huns enjoy following courageous leaders who aren't afraid to make decisions and to fail once in a while as a result. If you have lost your courage, you can get back on track. Here's what you must do. Begin today to take the ordinary risks your Huns and I expect of you. Do not equivocate. It is better to be known for making a decision or two that led to trouble than to be indecisive. Also encourage your Huns, particularly those with fiery ambition, to take risks. They will fall off their horses from time to time, but riding beside you is worth an occasional fall. Become neither discouraged nor bitter should you again be cruelly penalized for taking chances appropriate to your job. Moreover, don't try to get even. Instead, go to work for a chieftain who respects and rewards tribal leaders who dare to gamble, and remember, it is on the backs of the brave that the ordinary come to experience the pleasure of victory.

- **Denial Dependency**

Cowardly chieftains who dodge responsibility for their actions also direct scribes and sophists to deny their leader's culpability. The Huns see right through such subterfuge. Of course, Roman leaders have developed nonaccountability into a nasty but sophisticated joke on their people. But avoiding blame for having placed yourself or the tribe in a precarious situation is beneath the dignity of any chieftain worthy of being a Hun.

The most straightforward cure for denial dependency is to remove from office a chieftain who denies responsibility for his or her actions. A more novel cure is to compensate a chieftain's scapegoat with booty extracted from the guilty chieftain's own cache. Somehow, I think this second treatment would remedy the malady quickly enough. In the Hunnic nation, chieftains are paid to accept blame for their failures and those of their tribe. Huns are compensated only for what they do; for what they don't do, they get nothing. If, however, Huns are blamed for the shortcomings of their chieftain, I believe they should be compensated accordingly.

- **Empathy Amnesia**

Chieftains who are overanxious to impress the king with their ability to get the job done often forget why the job is being done in the first place. The only reason that we have jobs to do as leaders is to improve the present and secure a fine future for all Huns. A chieftain who thoughtlessly does his or her duties to bedazzle me (or other chieftains) but places the well-being of other Huns in jeopardy is infected with empathy amnesia. You have this disease if you fail to consider even the most remote implications in human terms of the way you and your Huns earn both glory and booty.

This illness is widespread but curable. If ultimately, you are hurting one Hun or many Huns, ask yourself why. What do you gain from destructive activities? If you gain power or bonus booty, then something is seriously wrong with our system of rewards—and you should help me fix it fast. The majority of Huns should not be made to suffer while their leaders increase their own booty and privilege. If, however, you are doing something I've asked of you, tell me that a course correction needs to be made. Tribal leaders are responsible for factoring in the short- and long-term costs of all tribal activities.

- **Factual Paranoia**

Although factual paranoia is more often present in young chieftains than in mature tribal leaders, it can chronically afflict insecure chieftains of any age. Infected leaders become pervasively suspicious of other Huns, whom they perceive to be out to trick them, dupe them, or usurp their power. And once in a while, they are right, for there are such Huns. Every chieftain really is someone's target. A few of your people will indeed seek to prejudice your decisions in their favor, while others will try to overthrow you. Sometimes these are the same people. But they are not as numerous as loyal Huns.

Factual paranoia is a difficult syndrome for a chieftain to overcome. Solving conflicts within the tribe requires perspective if you are to avoid becoming argumentative, stubborn, and defensive. You should always deal with any Hun who genuinely threatens your authority. Some need merely to be told that you know what they're up to and that you expect them to change their ways. Others will be so defiant that you must force them out of the tribe. Chieftains should always keep an open mind. Most Huns are not out to diminish their chieftain's authority.

Consider what positions need to be filled by people you absolutely trust, and then put trustworthy Huns in those jobs. Allow your key advisors and close associates the opportunity to win your confidence. They need it to be effective in their jobs. Most importantly, be a good chieftain and do not threaten the security of your Huns; they, in turn, are likely to be of little threat to yours.

- **Failure Phobia**

If you are so afraid of failing that you avoid activities in which you aren't guaranteed success, you are a victim of failure phobia. You are overly cautious, shun appropriate risks, and settle for mediocrity because it is safe.

Failure phobia is easily prevented. Young Huns should be

taught that it is acceptable to fail sometimes, especially on a first attempt. They should also be assured that they will excel at a few things, do well at many more, and be average or even below average in others. This is the natural state of Huns. They must learn to challenge their limits without dread of falling short. They should set their standards high —but not unreasonably so.

Any afflicted chieftain here present should remember that when you avoid failure, you sacrifice the possibility of success. We all should fear and confront real emotional and physical dangers. But you admit your irrational fears, study their causes, and find ways to eliminate them. In other words, free yourself and your Huns to accept challenges and take risks.

• Focus Neurosis
In the daily life of every chieftain, giving in to distractions from the goals of the tribe is an easy sickness to catch. I myself have had it once or twice, and it was costly indeed. Anything that takes your focus off tribal goals conflicts with reality, wastes time, consumes resources, and creates anxiety as you fall behind in your action plan.

Curing a serious case of focus neurosis is difficult, because most chieftains are too stubborn or too proud to admit they temporarily lose sight of their objectives. And by the time it comes to my attention that one of you chieftains is having a bout with focus neurosis, the damage has already been done to the nation. Therefore, preventing focus neurosis is the best course. I believe that healthy diversions refresh and recharge us all with the energy and devotion we need to achieve our goals. Such diversions should be brief, refreshing, fun—and conscious. Recognize the respite for what it is, and should you still have a problem in concentrating on tribal goals, tell me at once. I am not a happy Hun when something wrong is brought to my attention that is too late to do anything about.

- **Frontal Lobe Fixation**

This strange disease afflicts leaders who think that they are more intelligent than anyone below them in the tribe and that their brilliance increases with each promotion. Frontal lobe fixation causes the Huns to avoid you because they don't like being tuned out or being told they are stupid. When required to communicate with you, they will simply spoon-feed you your own ideas. Either way, everybody loses.

Chieftains with frontal lobe fixation can only be cured by exposure to leaders who themselves are infected by this disease. When victims see how great a problem frontal lobe fixation is in other leaders, they may recognize it as something to correct in themselves. If this treatment fails, their tribes are stuck with know-it-all leaders who in reality know less and accomplish less than if they drew on the intelligence around them.

- **Inflamed Ego**

Some chieftains labor under the illusion that they achieved high rank through their own efforts alone. Those among you who believe that, by becoming a chieftain, you simply fulfilled your destiny should wake up. Your persistent delusion of self-importance is a poor compensation for being firmly grounded in reality. You will never be a truly outstanding leader of Huns unless your inflamed ego recovers from its abnormally swollen state.

If you don't act quickly, the Huns may act for you. They are quick to jump at the first opportunity to humiliate overbearing, pompous leaders.

The prognosis for chieftains who have a chronic case of inflamed ego is poor, because they really believe their delusion. They lack insight. All successful leaders have been helped by teachers, mentors, and more capable leaders willing to take a chance on their unproven skills. Shock treatment is the only cure for an advanced case of inflamed ego: All support is precipitously withdrawn from the afflicted chieftain. Any chieftain with the slightest hold on reality quickly realizes how important Huns, warriors, and other chieftains were and are to his or her success. But shock treatment usually has devastating consequences, for the victim can rarely reverse his or her fortune within the same tribe and must move on to another.

Less fortunate chieftains suffering from inflamed ego do not receive shock treatments. Support is gradually withdrawn from them. The realization that they are nothing without the help of others arrives only after their confidence has withered. They have lost not only the ability to turn things around in their own tribe but also the confidence necessary to begin anew in another tribe.

• Insensitivity Complex
High-powered chieftains often become so engrossed in their duties that they overlook the interests of the Huns who report to them. This is not always bad. Chieftains need a certain insensitivity to make tough decisions that hurt some Huns directly under their command but ensure the larger good of the tribe and nation. Insensitivity complex becomes a serious problem when no amount of suffering among the Huns beneath the chieftain bothers him or her.

One remedy for this malady is for a chieftain to appoint advisors that won't be afraid to speak up when life gets difficult for subordinate Huns. Another remedy is for these Huns to revolt—a cure I don't believe you'll want to risk.

• Invulnerability Illusion
Which of you chieftains believes yourself to be so politically savvy, powerful, and indispensable that you can do whatever you will with impunity? To you I say, this is idiotic thinking. All of us gathered here tonight are vulnerable. Some of us will fall victim to our own shortcomings; others will be brought down by external forces. The fortunate, who prevail despite both, will reject fantasies that they are invincible.

Chieftains, you are assailable. Develop your weaknesses into strengths, and moderate your shortcomings, so they don't become stumbling blocks. If you still have hallucinations of invulnerability, my only suggestion is that you drink less wine.

• Loose Lips
A few chieftains disclose confidential information about plans, conditions, or people to impress others with their insider information or to make someone else look bad. This vicious and reckless practice is detrimental to the tribe and can destroy you as well as other Huns. Since the information being disclosed is either sensitive or sensational, the chieftain has an attentive audience and gets temporary glee from feeling important. The high soon passes, so the addicted chieftain has to divulge similar information to feed his or her habit. This addiction takes hold only in spineless tribal leaders, and I don't expect many of you to succumb to it.

Keeping confidential information to themselves earns chieftains the trust and respect of other tribal leaders as well as of the Huns. A trusted and respected chieftain is more effective than one from whom followers withhold information in order to protect it. Once a tribal leader becomes infected with this insidious disease, the cure may involve excising him or her from office.

• Omnipotence Obsession
A few among you are consumed by the desire for absolute power. You have yet to learn that you get things done by sharing authority with subordinate leaders acting on your behalf. This illness, like others, can alienate your subordinate leaders and Huns. They not only will avoid you, but also will find ways to show you that you are fallible. Recognizing you as the pompous ass you are, they will go to extremes to distract you from your goals.

The best cure is prevention. Chieftains should not promote Huns with symptoms of this disease to positions of tribal leadership. Promoting infected Huns endangers the health of the tribe. If prevention fails, alert me to the presence of an infected leader, and I will replace him or her with an able subordinate.

- **Popularity Paralysis**
Among those assembled here are some who won't make the tough, unpopular decisions required from time to time of all leaders. When a wise decision is unlikely to be graciously received by the Huns, you refuse to make it, which is unacceptable. While desiring social approval is normal, chieftains are expected to make unpopular decisions that are good for their tribes. Remember that making poor but popular decisions leads to unpopularity when the poor results of those decisions finally catch up with you.

Reversing the course of popularity paralysis is difficult. Chieftains who are so concerned with popularity and social approval that they can't make tough decisions should step aside. But those of you able to mature will find that life goes on regardless of which Huns like or dislike your decisions. And more importantly, you will find it much easier to live with yourself and with me when you have the courage to make the right decisions.

- **Predatory Inclination**
This minor illness can develop into sadistic gratification. It begins in an insecure chieftain who picks on wounded Huns instead of helping them heal. Such chieftains find sinister pleasure in attacking the weak. This distasteful distraction gives them a false sense of superiority. A truly superior chieftain never diminishes any Hun who stands in need.

Chieftains who assail the weak have two choices. The first choice is to immediately refrain from such behavior and hope that I never find out about it. The second is to be removed by me from the tribe as a possible carrier capable of transmitting sadistic gratification. Although my treatment of this disease is harsh, contagion must be stopped before it spreads.

• Productivity Charade

Some of you chieftains think you fool me by pursuing activities that you enjoy and are competent in but that don't make meaningful contributions to your tribes or our nation. Well, you are the fools. Your productivity charade may confuse others, but not me. Your tribes should engage in work that contributes to the well-being of the Huns and the nation. If you are using your resources toward any other end, you are afflicted with productivity charade and will soon be exposed.

The cure for this illness is inspection. It is the nature of Huns to dally when they don't believe anyone cares enough to check on them. A chieftain should always inspect the work of his or her tribal leaders to be sure they are doing their assigned tasks. And as your king, I will continue to inspect your work as chieftains.

• Recognition Rigor Mortis

A chieftain who resents another's accomplishments, or who becomes defensive when his or her achievements are not constantly heralded, has come down with recognition rigor mortis. Allowed to run its course, recognition rigor mortis compels a chieftain to undermine the accomplishments of subordinates and even to steal their moments of glory. You chieftains should know that this makes deserving Huns and their friends really mad. The possibility of a mass revolt against your unscrupulous abuse of authority is neither attractive nor unlikely.

Truly successful chieftains never catch recognition rigor mortis, for they know that some of their significant accomplishments may go unnoticed. They do not compete with their Huns for recognition. They understand that acknowledging subordinates is in everyone's best interest and tells the Huns which accomplishments are admired. As a result,

Huns headed in other directions can begin to emulate their winning colleagues. So don't compete with your Huns for recognition, and don't withhold earned rewards from your Huns. But do not praise the Huns for just doing their jobs either. Getting by may be a big deal for the Romans, but in the world of the Huns, it is mediocrity.

• Sadistic Gratification

A chieftain who is a bully will not merely get rid of a vulnerable adversary within the tribe but will make the victim suffer unnecessarily. Moreover, when this powerful thrill seeker wants to gratify a sadistic urge, he or she may seek out an innocent and helpless victim if no adversary is available.

This despicable behavior will not be tolerated. Those among you who manifest the slightest symptom of this dreadful disease should understand that I do not believe there to be a cure for it. My procedure for eliminating sadistic gratification is to decisively and immediately eliminate any culprit who indulges in it. Need I say more?

• Suffering Syndrome

This disorder is a false but chronic conviction that the Huns are most productive when they suffer. Afflicted chieftains avoid suffering with their Huns even if it is necessary, and they don't take action to end the Huns' unhappiness. As soon as the Huns realize either that their distress is artificially induced or that it is borne alone, they sabotage the efforts of the tribe. They also find ways (subtle and overt) to make their mean-spirited chieftain suffer, too.

Suffering syndrome is an easy disease for a chieftain to avoid. Just remember that miserable Huns never perform at their best. You don't have to experiment with this idea. I have told you how it is, and that is sufficient. If you want peak performance from your Huns—which you do as long as I am king—create peak conditions for them. If this means that you yourself suffer a little in making life better for your Huns, so much the better. You will end up appreciating them more, and when Huns are appreciated by their chieftain, they work harder to perform at the top of their form.

And so I conclude my lecture on the common diseases of chieftainship and their cures. I did not discuss innocuous maladies because I want you to focus on the critical. I also want my words to be clearly understood, so I did not coat them with honey or interject diplomatic praise for inept leadership. I, Attila, admit that some of the diseases I have described tonight have infected me briefly. I must work to maintain good health in mind as well as body. I expect no less from you. Perfection in leadership is an ideal to move toward—it is not a goal I expect myself or you to reach. Your dreams should always exceed your grasp. The day in which you cannot see ways to improve your own performance is the day you should resign. I admonish you to take a few moments at sunrise and at sunset to reflect on these guiding principles for having a long and successful career as a leader:

• Keep a sense of humor about yourself. You'll never be truly successful if you take yourself too seriously, and the Huns don't work hard for a sourpuss.

• Stay mentally flexible. Rigidity of mind inhibits your own progress and that of the tribe.

• Develop good relationships with your Huns. If you don't understand your Huns, and they don't understand you, not much will get done.

• Focus on helping the Huns, not yourself. Bringing out the best in your Huns and promoting their well-being are the best ways to excel as their leader.

• Maintain your balance: mind, body, and heart; public life and private life; solitude and community; work and recreation.

- Enjoy whatever you do, but avoid complacency. Remember that you will never become highly accomplished in activities you do not enjoy. Find something you like to do—that the Huns need done—and give it your best.

As you leave this great assembly, know that you are not only my chieftains but also my comrades. We take risks together, suffer with each other, and prosper from our mutual support of a cause that is greater than any one of us alone. Long live the Huns!

EPILOGUE

"Exit the Huns"

Because of the setback at Châlons in 451 and the Italian campaign in early 452, Attila's approval rating plummeted. No sooner had the king of Huns returned to Etzelnburg from the Italian peninsula in 452 than he learned that some of his allies were claiming independence from the Hunnic confederacy. Moreover, for the first time, he faced dissent in his own family: Attila's sons were impatient with him for promising them their own kingdoms but not delivering. For his part, the king of Huns was disappointed that his Great Conquest was moving so slowly. He decided a new campaign was in order to win back his sons and reestablish unity in his Hunnic confederacy. The Great Conquest could only continue, however, after disaffected members of the confederacy repledged themselves to the cause.

Attila decided the time had come to accept the challenge of Marcian, emperor of the Eastern Roman Empire at Constantinople. Marcian had, on succeeding Theodosius to the throne, abruptly stopped paying the tribute that Attila had negotiated with Constantinople in return for peace. Furthermore, Marcian had sent word to Attila that if he wanted the gold, he would have to come and get it. For almost two years, Attila had let the matter slide. Now, to Attila's way of thinking, it was a good enough pretext for war. He announced in the spring of 452 that the Huns would begin a new expedition against the East.

Because the unity he had worked so hard to achieve was

still tenuous, Attila chose carefully the tribes to be included
in his quickly reorganized army. He showed no mercy to
those he did not trust to march with him on Constantinople. While inspecting his German subjects, for instance,
Attila found that some of the tribes had declared independence from his confederacy. Attila dealt with the rebel
chieftains in the only way he believed would convince their
tribes to realign with him—he executed them.

Ildico, an extraordinarily beautiful daughter of one such
rebel chieftain, begged Attila to spare her father's life. The
king of Huns ignored her pleas but noted her beauty. After
ordering her father's execution, Attila took Ildico back to
Etzelnburg, where he announced he would marry her. The
expedition against Marcian would begin after the wedding.

The marriage of the king of Huns to a young bride was
thought by the Huns to foreshadow a joyous future. They
held a great wedding celebration for Attila and Ildico, at-
tended by many kings, chieftains, and nobles from among
his allies.

After the wedding ceremony, tribal chieftains presented
the newlyweds with mare's milk in wooden vessels (a traditional gesture). Guests heaped wedding presents before the
couple—jewels, purple cloth, embroidered silks, fine saddles, rugs, bronze vases, paintings, and ivory statues. During
the feast that followed, wine flowed freely. In an unusual
indulgence, Attila drank a wooden goblet filled with wine in
honor of each one of his distinguished guests, and as there
were many of them, the king of Huns was drunk by the time
he and his young bride made their way to the wooden hut
that served as their nuptial chamber.

When, by the middle of the next day, the bridal couple
had not appeared, Edecon knocked at the door of their hut.
No response. Afraid that something was terribly wrong,
Edecon sent for Attila's sons and ministers. None of them
could decide what to do, so without further hesitation,
Edecon broke the door's lock. He, Onegesius, Attila's sons,
and the royal bodyguard entered the hut. Their king lay

naked and motionless on the bed in a pool of his own blood. Ildico shivered in a corner, staring wide-eyed at nothing. The king of Huns was dead! Ildico never spoke again.

There are three versions of how Attila died. One is that his sons had him assassinated because he hadn't given them their promised kingdoms. But they were probably too smart to choose such a risky time and place to kill the king of Huns, and furthermore, Attila did not raise sons capable of patricide. Another version is that Ildico killed Attila to avenge his execution of her father. Since no signs of a bodily wound or poison were found, this version is possible but not probable. The third version is that he died from a cerebral hemorrhage—perhaps brought on by too much wedding-night excitement. In any event, Attila, king of Huns, passed away in 453 at the age of fifty-eight.

Attila had united hundreds of incongruous tribes in a great Hunnic confederacy, which became the dominant power in the barbarian world during his lifetime. In an interesting parallel, Aëtius had saved the Western Roman Empire from total disintegration during his lifetime. The armies of these two contemporary leaders had fought as allies and also had battled as enemies. Aëtius was murdered by the emperor Valentinian III in 454. Whether fate or coincidence, Aëtius, like Attila, was fifty-eight years old at the time of his death.

The two men, who respected each other, were personally ambitious but fought for causes larger than self-interest. Yet neither man achieved his ultimate goal. Attila's Great Conquest was never completed. Aëtius' attempt to reunite the Roman Empire and restore its former glory failed. In fact, the Hunnic confederacy and the Western Roman Empire both fell before the end of the fifth century. *Sic transit gloria mundi.*

Selected Bibliography

Boak, Arthur E. R. *A History of Rome to 565 A.D.*, 4th ed. New York: The Macmillan Company, 1955.

Brion, Marcel. *Attila, the Scourge of God*, trans. Harold Ward. New York: Robert M. McBride & Company, 1929.

Durant, Will. *The Story of Civilization*, vol. 4, *The Age of Faith*. New York: Simon and Schuster, 1950.

Eggenberger, David. *An Encyclopedia of Battles: Accounts of over 1,560 Battles from 1479 B.C. to the Present.* New York: Dover Publications, Inc., 1985.

Ferrill, Arther. *The Fall of the Roman Empire: The Military Explanation.* New York: Thames and Hudson, Inc., 1986.

Gibbon, Edward. *Decline and Fall of the Roman Empire*, vol. 3. London: Everyman's Library, 1910.

Gordon, C. D. *The Age of Attila: Fifth-Century Byzantium and the Barbarians.* Ann Arbor, Mich.: Ann Arbor Paperbacks, The University of Michigan Press, 1966.

Grant, Michael. *The Roman Emperors.* New York: Charles Scribner's Sons, 1985.

Hadas, Moses, and the editors of Time-Life Books. *Imperial Rome.* New York: Time, Inc., 1965.

Hoyt, Robert S., and Stanley Chodorow. *Europe in the Middle Ages,* 3rd ed. Orlando, Fla.: Harcourt Brace Jovanovich, Inc., 1985.

Lewis, Naphtali, and Meyer Reinhold, eds. *Roman Civilization: Selected Readings,* vol. 2, *The Empire.* New York: Columbia University Press, 1990.

Maechen-Helfen, Otto J. *The World of the Huns: Studies in Their History and Culture,* ed. Max Knight. Berkeley, Calif.: University of California Press, 1973.

Muhlberger, Steven. *The Fifth-Century Chroniclers: Prosper, Hydatius and the Gallic Chronicler of 452.* Leeds, England: Francis Cairns (Publications) Ltd., 1990.

Musset, Lucien. *The Germanic Invasions,* trans. Edward and Columba James. London: Elek Books, Ltd., 1975.

Newark, Tim. *The Barbarians.* Dorset, England: Blandford Press, 1985.

Niebuhr, B. G. *Lectures on Roman History Delivered at the University of Bonn,* vol. 3, trans. Le M. Havilland, M. A. Chepmell, and F. C. F. Demmler. London: Henry G. Bohn, 1855.

Previte-Orton, C. W. *The Shorter Cambridge Medieval History,* vols. 1 and 2. Cambridge, England: Cambridge University Press, 1952.

Simons, Gerald, and the editors of Time-Life Books. *Barbarian Europe.* New York: Time-Life Books, 1968.

Strayer, Joseph R. *Western Europe in the Middle Ages.* New York: Appleton-Century-Crofts, Inc., 1955.

Suskind, Richard. *The Barbarians.* New York: W.W. Norton & Company, Inc., 1970.

Thompson, E. A. *A History of Attila and the Huns.* London: Oxford University Press, 1948.

Todd, Malcolm. *Everyday Life of the Barbarians: Goths, Franks and Vandals.* New York: Dorset Press, 1972.

Windrow, Martin. *The Invaders.* New York: ARCO Publishing, Inc., 1979.

Wolfram, Herwig. *History of the Goths,* trans. Thomas J. Dunlap. Berkeley, Calif.: University of California Press, 1988.